Praise for Hilary Yancey

"Hilary's work is true in the best Christian sense: She brings order out of chaos, finds beauty out of brokenness, participates in redemption out of sorrow, and practices resurrection in the very places of death. Her writing has an inexplicable loveliness to each word, like we're all homesick for what she glimpsed."

—Sarah Bessey, author of *Jesus Feminist* and *Out of Sorts: Making Peace with an Evolving Faith*

"Hilary is one of my favorite writers. Period. Because she's not afraid of what her writing will uncover. She's not afraid to look doubt and question marks and God in the eye. And then she's not afraid to tell us exactly what she found. Open this book and let her show you. I promise it will change you too."

—Lisa-Jo Baker, author of *Never Unfriended* and *Surprised by Motherhood*

"With poetry and insight, authenticity and vulnerability, Hilary explores the hidden work of making space. Space for the stories we never thought would be ours. Space for the people who become ours to love. Space for the Grace of God that so often lies hidden under it all."

—Addie Zierman, author of *When We Were on Fire* and *Night Driving*

"Hilary Yancey's writing is fraught with humanity and divinity, both. Her words are full of the ... beautiful infusion of wisdom that happens when life does what it does."

—Amber C. Haines, author of *Wild in the Hollow*

FORGIVING
GOD

A STORY OF FAITH

HILARY YANCEY

New York Nashville

FaithWords
Hachette Book Group
1290 Avenue of the Americas, New York, NY 10104
faithwords.com
twitter.com/faithwords

First Edition: April 2018

FaithWords is a division of Hachette Book Group, Inc. The FaithWords name and logo are trademarks of Hachette Book Group, Inc.

The publisher is not responsible for websites (or their content) that are not owned by the publisher.

The Hachette Speakers Bureau provides a wide range of authors for speaking events. To find out more, go to www.hachettespeakersbureau.com or call (866) 376-6591.

Library of Congress Control Number: 2017959712

ISBNs: 978-1-5460-3299-1 (hardcover), 978-1-5460-3300-4 (ebook)

Printed in the United States of America

LSC-C

10 9 8 7 6 5 4 3 2 , 1

To Jack, who looks like Jesus,
and to Preston, who built the ark

FORGIVING GOD

THE JORDAN RIVER

I learned I was pregnant after an argument. "Is this even real coffee?" I asked angrily after taking a small sip from the mug Preston, my husband, had just placed in front of me.

"Yes?" Preston looked at me quizzically.

We kept only regular coffee in the house, never decaf, so it was an odd question to ask. In response, I burst into tears.

Alarmed, Preston asked, "What's really going on?"

I mumbled something about being sure I would fail all my graduate classes that semester and probably something about how I was the worst philosopher I'd ever met. I can't remember exactly what I said next, but I remember Preston taking a step back, leaning up against the sink, and asking, "Should you take a pregnancy test?"

The thought hadn't occurred to me. I shot Preston what I hoped was a withering look and marched into the bathroom. In defiance, I took the spare test we kept under the sink, prepared to prove that I was being the reasonable person, thank you, and my tears had nothing to do with something as wild or uncontrolled as hormones. The pregnancy test is meant to take a full two minutes, but the plus sign appeared after a handful of seconds. I glanced down while drying my hands and there he was. The pink lines kept deepening as the seconds ticked by, a faint pink quickly turning almost magenta, as if someone kept retracing the lines with a marker. My son Jackson has been forceful in proclaiming his existence ever since.

When I opened the bathroom door, Preston was on the couch, listening to the soundtrack to a musical called *Violet*. The title character was belting out a refrain from "On My Way" as I walked to the coffee table and perched on it, holding the test.

> *Left my troubles all behind me*
> *Back there when I climbed on board*
> *Jordan River's where you'll find me*
> *It's wide but not too wide to ford.*

Violet is the story of a girl who wants to be healed—physically healed. It's a story about faces that look different and the hope that those faces might change. It's a story about the miracles we ask for, even when we don't ask out loud.

We listened to the soundtrack on repeat that first morning of our changed life. Sutton Foster sang us to the CVS for extra tests. We drove down the highways of Waco, our voices joining the cast. We wondered if it was a boy or a girl. We wondered where we would fit a crib in our studio apartment. We laughed about the fight over coffee. Sutton Foster belted that refrain—*Jordan River's where you'll find me*—but we didn't feel anywhere close to that river or the story she sang.

A few months into our pregnancy with Jackson, we received a phone call. The nurse's thin voice slipped out of the speakers on my phone, and with it words: words with medical definitions, *cleft lip and palate*, *follow-up ultrasound*, *high-risk pregnancy*. Now, when I lean up against the bricks of the room where I first heard those words, they echo back, the walls keeping a record of the moment that everything changed. From there we had ultrasounds—what felt like hundreds, but what I now know was only nine. The maternal-fetal medicine specialist ordered a fetal MRI, an unusual procedure, attempting to understand our son's face. There were second and third phone calls. The news rolled in. Jackson had no right eye, a very small jaw and chin, no external ear. *Significant facial cleft*, they called it in the genetic counselor's office when we asked what language we should use to tell family and friends. I inhaled the words, and they filled my lungs with cold water, and it seemed that every breath for the next twenty weeks of my pregnancy came out like a gasp.

During those twenty weeks, between the first phone call and Jack's first breath, we drove hundreds of miles to and from the hospital, to and from each consultation, each proximate diagnosis. When we drove, we listened to songs about miracles. We listened to praise music from our childhoods, gospel choirs, and old hymns. We never played Sutton Foster's song, but we were still singing about the Jordan River. We were still singing about water that Jesus might walk on to come save us from what each appointment said was probably coming.

After Jack finally arrived, we lived forty-three days in the NICU, our hearts beating outside us in a blue, yellow, and red crib in what was labeled the Pink Room.

Jack had surgery just three weeks into his life to receive a tracheostomy and gastrostomy button (G-button)—his breathing and eating both to be done through tiny tubes nestled in tunnels of tissue carved by surgeons. We were scheduled for seventeen consultations—over three pages of appointments—before we were discharged. We drove home on a gray November morning too tired to think about singing. Jack slept, and for the first time since that twenty-week mark, I didn't have anything left to pray.

★ ★ ★

Jackson's first and favorite lullaby was "Poor Wayfaring Stranger." *I'm only goin' over Jordan / I'm only goin' over home.* He still falls asleep leaning against my chest as I sing. I tell him again and again that these are the songs of our family: We are traveling up to the river, to the edge of it, and somehow, out into the water itself. I whisper across the wisps of his blond hair that I do not know how we came here, how to measure the expectations we once had against the weight of the miracles we were given. Jesus was calling us all—"Even you, Jack," I say—to get out of the boat and come meet him. Meeting him, I promise Jack, is never what you once imagined.

Someone bought *The Jesus Storybook Bible* for Jack, and it says that when Jesus is sent from the Jordan River, it is the beginning of the Great Rescue. Jesus rises from the water to do works many could not have believed except that they had seen them. Some couldn't believe them even then. Jesus comes up from the river to meet us: wayfarers with just our toes at the edge of the water, trying to find our way. Jesus was sent away from the Jordan to bring us back to it. To make us get out onto the water, far beyond where we might have gone on our own, out where our feet can't touch the bottom. I'm coming to believe that's where we find God. In the river that's wide, but not too wide. That's where I am now, searching for him. That's where he took me, and where I brought myself.

This is a book about wading deep in the Jordan River— into those months where I prayed for miracles and the months that followed. This is a book about wading out in the confidence of one belief and finding that your feet can't touch the bottom, that you might not know how to swim, that it is harder to see Jesus than you first thought. This is a book about the death of old love and the labor of new. A book about God. A book about forgiveness.

Chapter 1

DIAGNOSIS

I was sitting just outside the philosophy office, at a round table, working on a set of logic problems when the department's office manager poked her head around the corner. She motioned me into the office and pointed to one of the phones, its red "hold" light flashing a steady rhythm. As a graduate student, I didn't have my own work phone, so on the OB-GYN intake form I had filled out sixteen weeks before, I had listed the philosophy office number. I had assumed no one ever called work phones. It was the OB-GYN office.

"Are you somewhere private?" I don't remember if the nurse said hello. I think she must have, because people usually do. But I only remember telling her no, I wasn't, and told her I'd call her back on my cell phone. I began

7

the work of worrying even as I dialed her number, which I'd written on a Post-it note. *Don't panic,* I told myself, and my heart replied, *You must.* As the phone rang, I began to pace around the open hallway so that no one could catch more than a few sentences. We had been told at our ultrasound a week before that we'd only receive a call if there was a problem; no news meant good news. I had waited the weekend, sure that the phone call would come. When Monday had finally come and gone, I felt relieved by the thought that our newly named Jackson was healthy and normal. The nurse's voice was rigid, almost metallic. She seemed to read the words off a piece of paper in front of her, no pauses, no punctuation.

"Your ultrasound results indicate that Baby has a cleft lip and palate do you know what these are?" *Baby* is a universal name for the person in the black-and-white pictures, the heartbeat you've been hearing for weeks, the long-awaited one, for our particularly long-awaited one. I started to cry, and, becoming embarrassed to be crying in front of the nurse delivering news that I had finally believed I would not get about my baby, I choked out a yes and told her I knew what they were. Hadn't I seen the infomercials?

They used to play on our small TV in the living room during special presentations of movies or documentaries. During that phone call, I pictured the videos, children looking at the camera, their eyes wide with joy and long-ing, mouths gaping and grinning, their lips twisted up or away, revealing thin strips of pink gums. This was all I thought about, and then I stopped thinking.

I stood in the hallway of my department on campus, holding my still-small belly, where I was longing to feel movement. The words were on a distant, scratchy loop that I couldn't turn off: *ultrasound Baby cleft lip palate correctable with surgery*. None of them computed; they floated past me but they kept returning. The words themselves were still following me. The nurse practitioner told me she didn't handle high-risk pregnancies; I would need a new ob-gyn. She told me I needed a follow-up ul-trasound with a maternal-fetal medicine specialist, asked whether I preferred to go to Temple or Dallas. She was still talking to me; I was a ghost holding the phone.

"Temple."

I said Temple. My mouth, disengaged from my empty brain, started to babble at top speed about how Temple was closer, which was so good because you know there is a lot of traffic on 35 and it would be too bad to drive to Dallas. When I finally stopped, she said she would put in the referral that day. I nodded, though she couldn't see me, and finally, after a lot of what she must have thought was silence on my part, she asked, "Are you okay?"

"Uh, yeah, just a little...overwhelmed, I guess." I

started to cry again, and so I told her I had to go, that I needed to call my husband. Preston came and picked me up, and when I sat down in the front seat, I stared at my hands in my lap, my book bag by my feet. "The nurse called. She said something is wrong with Jackson, that he has a cleft lip and a cleft palate. That's what the ultrasounds showed, and we have to go for a follow-up in Temple." Preston nodded, took deep breaths as he swung the car onto University Parks Drive.

That's what the ultrasounds showed. Even as I spoke those words, I hoped they could rescue us, that the nurse had just reported something that *looked* like cleft lip and palate. Another ultrasound, or three or four more, could show something different, could prove her wrong. I clung to the promise that seemed to rest in her words, that she was calling because of apparent test results, but the person behind them, he might defy the tests, he might prove us all wrong.

★ ★ ★

Before we knew about Jackson's diagnosis (before I was showing and he was a monthly appointment and heart-beats thudding wild in my belly), I downloaded the What to Expect When You're Expecting app. I read about the daily changes, waiting patiently every Tuesday morning for the weekly updates, with paragraphs of advice and things to think about. I wanted both glory and guilt; I wanted to know just what *should be happening* and what *I should be doing* to keep myself—so I thought—preparing to be a good mother. I *ought* to go to the gym. I *ought* to drink only decaffeinated tea. I *ought* to rest but also be active. Guilt, I have believed for far too long, is the safest, most reliable motivation for doing things you ought to do. I was driven by the fear of it and the feeling of it, to put in headphones and do Zumba in our apartment, to keep a record of how many vegetables and fruits I was eating.

But I went farther and farther down the rabbit hole each week. I read message boards and user threads and every post from every slightly panicked mother I could find. I soaked in the worries and their sly counterpart, the reassurances. A mother writes worried about morning sickness, and six other moms write back that, don't worry, *they had the same thing* and dear son and dear daughter turned out fine. Our nurse practitioner wrote down at my first appointment that we had a "large baby for gestational age," which prompted her to order an early ultrasound. I spent a week looking up every possible meaning of *large baby for gestational age*. I lay awake in bed replaying the possibilities from the crumbs scattered in forums and mom blogs. I fought with Preston about whether it was justified to be worried. He insisted it wasn't, that it didn't mean anything and probably our nurse just wanted to find a way to make insurance pay for the ultrasound, to do us a favor. When I thought he had fallen asleep, I looked up the blogs again on my phone, turning away from him so he wouldn't see. This is the secret work of those blogs, of What to Expect, of the app and the animated weekly baby growth update: They make any reassurance that's not from another mom, who's been through the same thing, sound hollow.

I drank and drank and drank at that well of worry and reassurance, each sip leaving me thirstier. I could not stop thinking about the thousands of things I could ask. Should I eat pineapples? I read somewhere they can bring on early labor by softening the cervix. Should I eat yogurt? How much should I work out, and when is prenatal yoga most likely to benefit the baby?

And this seemingly bottomless well offered me the same empty water—*well, I did Zumba and I highly recommend it. I did Zumba and had an early miscarriage. Have you taken time for a prenatal yoga class? Calcium is the most important thing, except for folic acid, which they tell you that your diet will provide but it probably won't and it's super important in the beginning of pregnancy, so you should have been taking a prenatal vitamin for about six weeks before you started trying to have a baby.*

I could not stop looking things up. I could not stop drinking in this promise that if my answers to these questions were the same as those posted by seven other moms, then the baby would be okay. I prayed desperately night after night that God would just not let anything happen to this baby.

I tried to hide the depths of my worry from Preston the whole first trimester by only opening the app and reading the threads of conversation after he had dropped me off at school for the morning. Then I would settle in with my phone and my computer to learn what should be happening with the little one I was carrying. By now he should have arm and leg buds. By now he should have a heart beating strongly, forming its four chambers. Every day there was another "tip" for moms—ways to process what we were feeling or thinking or how to avoid morning sickness. Every week another animated graphic of what "Baby" looks like. Every week a reminder to think about things like dream nursery boards and flu shots and finding the "right" ob-gyn or midwife.

There is a strange superiority in this work of worrying and reassuring. We complain about the things that actually make us feel better. We *want* morning sickness while we complain about how awful it is. But we are secretly pleased to have it, because, you know, not having it could mean that your little one is having trouble. Sick mom, healthy baby. I don't know how many women will say, *I didn't have any morning sickness and everything was fine!* but I doubt it will ever stop up the flood, because it only takes one woman to whisper, to hint, that it is a sign of trouble and away we run back to the well, back to the chaos, back to the worry.

I did this. I took comfort in the fact that I couldn't stomach anything before 11:00 a.m. I took comfort in seeing my applesauce or my yogurt come back up in the mornings. *This means the baby is okay.* I lived in the uneasy reassurance that my experience was "normal" and so the baby would be too. I read the blog posts, tried to follow their advice, collapsed into bed each night afraid that I had done something to put the baby, no bigger than a blueberry, in mortal danger, calmed only by one last quick look: *If I drank wine at a wedding before I knew I was pregnant, will everything be okay?*

★ ★ ★

In the first days after the phone call, we thought Jackson probably had a genetic condition of some kind, a twist or turn in that double helix that would have necessarily surfaced, no matter what I did or didn't do. Pierre Robin sequence is a range of genetic duplications or deletions, spontaneous edits to the text of our growing bodies. The maternal-fetal medicine specialist, Dr. D, suggested it as a possibility, since it usually presents with malformations of the chin and jaw, with cleft lip and palate. But he couldn't tell us, and the genetic counselors couldn't tell us, what had really happened. Of the hundreds of thousands of bits of sequences that can change, all of us have something slightly different. Somewhere in the joining of chromosomes, our genes write the story a bit differently. It's only in a few cases that the story becomes more complicated, only a fragment of the many hundreds of changes that make the doctors look longer, double-check measurements, send you to an office with too-brightly-colored plastic play mats.

We learned later, in the NICU, that it wasn't genetic. The right side of Jackson's face had been positioned in such a way, early on, that the blood didn't flow enough to keep pace with his growth. Everything slowed down, the eye, the ear—they were made in miniature or not made at all. The body builds creatively; the body builds in the windows and spaces it is given. For one moment, a small pearl of time, there wasn't enough blood, and so the body shifted and slowed and this beautiful face, so different from what we expected, took on the shape it has now.

I had imagined I would leave the geneticist's office feeling absolved. I had weighed in secret a dangerous hope that Jackson's condition *was* genetic. I imagined that if it was the dark and mysterious DNA that caused this, and not me, I could exhale. We hadn't expected to get pregnant so soon. I hadn't been reading those user threads about what to do when you are trying to conceive, and though we had known, that crisp Christmas Eve night, in the same darkness of spirit where God says *light*, that it was time to try, to receive, I hadn't prepared. I drank champagne at a wedding. We flew to Belgium and back and I drank wine there and I never thought about folic acid. I never thought about vitamins, calcium, the preparation of my body to become a mother.

So I prayed the dangerous prayer that Jack's condition would be genetic so that the DNA could absolve me of my inattention, my failings so early on to be the mother the user threads described. And the geneticist told me that there would be no absolution that way. I carried the guilt of the champagne for months; it was not until much later, sitting in a different hospital while Jack slept on my chest, sick with respiratory syncytial virus (RSV), that I wondered for the first time if I was seeking absolution for what only the internet called sin.

★ ★ ★

We were late to our eighteen-week ultrasound. Preston surprised me with a lunch date at a farm-to-table restaurant just outside Waco. I had been picking at my salad throughout, then picking at my dessert. Ever since the positive pregnancy test, ever since the scribbled note of "large baby for gestational age," I had lived on a live wire of worry. This ultrasound, which was the reason for the lunch, the reason for the celebrating, was full of fear. An ultrasound could declare that things hadn't gone according to plan or it could bless us with uneventful normalcy, with everything as expected. I had worried for days that it would be the first, and as the ultrasound approached, I became convinced that something *was* wrong, that we would learn something terrible that Friday afternoon. I sat sullenly at our celebration lunch, listlessly moving the lettuce around on my plate with my fork. Preston tried several times to ask me why I didn't seem very peaceful or excited. He tried to remind me that we were seeing our child for the first time. Instead of answering his question, I picked a fight with him about the fact that we would be late right as the waitress brought over our check. It was raining while we drove back, and I wasn't dressed for it. My thin cotton skirt was covered in wet splotches. I pressed my hands against it, feeling a thousand goose bumps beneath.

We arrived and I was called back fairly quickly. Preston stood up to join me, but the nurse told him to wait, that they would "call Dad back later." I followed the nurse silently, holding my wallet in my hands because my skirt didn't have any pockets. Once I was on the table, the technician started to swirl the transducer probe over my belly only to declare irritably that she couldn't see much because my bladder was too full, and gestured to a bathroom across the narrow hallway. I stood up and walked meekly to the bathroom. I was mad that I had been late, mad that I had tried so hard to drink the eight necessary glasses of water a day only to be told it was wrong. I am the kind of person who, upon deciding that she has done the entire day wrong, cannot be persuaded otherwise. I had failed the morning; I had failed lunch with my husband; I had failed the ultrasound; I had failed this baby. I washed my hands and slunk back into the room.

The exam was completely silent. The technician commented only once, to express frustration that the baby moved so much that she was having trouble getting good pictures of the face. She sighed multiple times, tracing the same circles around and around, shifting in her chair. When she said that the baby was so active, I tried to smile. "That's good, right?" She said nothing. I continued to stare at the green-and-cream border on the walls. There was a large calendar just opposite the exam table, turned to the month of April. It was a calendar with platitudes written across a beautiful sunrise background, things like "Live, laugh, love" and "Every act of kindness grows the spirit and strengthens the soul," things people put up on refurbished shiplap in their homes. I read the words on the April graphic of a generic sunrise, or a sweetly blooming daffodil, and swallowed too loudly. I wondered if she could hear my heart beating against my bones. I wondered if she was judging me, my silence, my lack of questions or exclamations or rambunctious joy. I wondered if she had even registered my face before hunting for my child's.

I prayed in that room, lying in that anxious horizontal position, my hands tickled by the paper they roll onto exam tables. God spoke one thing back, something I have forgotten until the writing of this book, something I proclaimed for a week or two, until the diagnosis, until the end and the beginning: "She can never tell you something about this person I do not already know."

When we think about God's foreknowledge, we are tempted to run so far out, foreknowledge trailing behind us like a kite. We cannot do, say, think, *be* anything but what God has already seen, already ordained, already determined. We think in terms of past, and present, and future, and God contains them all in his knowledge, a bucket of truths about us. We think, *God already knows*, and we often translate this as *God already made it to be the case that . . .* or *God already did*. At least we think, *It can't be anything except this.*

But I think God's foreknowledge might be better understood as an action. God foreknows because he is in all the places where we will go, because he stands next to us and near us before and after we get there. He hovers over and in and through time, and here the descriptions feel thin, unable to pin down the truth. God stands where we will stand. God moves where we will move. God sees what we do not yet but will someday see.

The summer I was pregnant with Jackson, as I studied for comprehensive exams in ancient and medieval philosophy, I read St. Augustine and Boethius on the question of foreknowledge. They wondered, together, despite the years between them, about how foreknowledge and freedom coincide. Boethius writes, in the voice of Lady Philosophy, that "human reason cannot approach the immediacy of the divine knowledge." God is in an eternal present, looking forth, a familiarity, a closeness with what we call future. God is immediate with the future. *She can never tell you something about this person I do not already know.* We are quick to think that because God knew, God caused, or because God knew, God made it that way, that it could not be different, that God had already planned it all. We wonder why, if God knew something was going to happen, he didn't intervene. Why didn't he change the results of that ultrasound? Why didn't he prevent what he already knew was coming?

But if we imagine that this knowledge God has about things we do not know is more like God seeing, God standing somewhere and understanding things we haven't yet learned, I wonder whether this might give us room to breathe. I wonder whether we might stop trying to work out the calculus of causation, how God fits nicely into the narrative, how to make sense of suffering if it's true that God already knows the suffering. Maybe it doesn't mean that God caused it in that simple way we often like to pretend. Maybe it just means that God has already experienced the suffering, stood in the midst of it, known you in the midst of it, known your heart, known its breaking. Maybe it is also true, then, that God has known its mending, that he joins these experiences together in the immediacy of his knowing.

The idea of a normal pregnancy died on that table, in the quiet, before the technician brought Preston back. It must have died long before, at the time the ideas about pregnancy should die—when the child arrives, when the pregnancy begins. I didn't know it then. Then, I only knew that God had said his knowing was more immediate and perfect than the unfriendly technician. I knew that when Preston came back and she turned the screen around, our boy wiggled and rolled three or four times in thirty seconds, that it was "definitely" a boy, that he was definitely ours, that I loved every tiny highlighted bone and every mysterious piece of him moving through me. I knew that we would name him Jackson David, which means "God has been gracious" and "beloved friend." I knew we would laugh and cry about how we had thought Jackson was a girl for all these weeks. My normal pregnancy died with the annunciation: God has been gracious; God has given us a gift, a beloved friend.

No one would ever tell us anything about Jackson that God did not already know.

Chapter 2

AFTERMATH

The morning of our follow-up appointment, I had become strangely confident that Jackson did not actually have a cleft lip and palate. This confidence astonished and intimidated me, and I worked hard to dismiss it. We drove to Temple for the first time, and as we passed semis and cars going too slow for Preston's taste on the road that morning, I wondered aloud. Had God, perhaps, already done a miracle? Was Jesus already moving, through the special Eucharistic service we had had the previous Sunday? Through the prayers we knew covered all three of us from so many far-flung places?

We followed the directions, found the 3A desk, checked in, traced our way back down the maze of side hallways to the octagon-shaped room where we waited for the ultrasound technician. A nurse took my blood pressure and my weight and brought us back to a room with a large TV where we could see Jack lit up, larger than life. The ultrasound itself was an hour long, the technician hovering over the same few spots on my stomach to try to snatch a picture of Jackson when he wiggled by. She thanked us at the end and left, saying only that the doctor would be in once he had looked at the scans.

It was a full thirty minutes before we met Dr. D. He apologized for the wait, told us that he had been looking at the scans in detail. He asked what we knew about why we were here.

We had prayed in the car that we would be told it was nothing, a mistake in the first ultrasound, that Jack was okay and that we could return to normal life. I thought about telling Dr. D that we weren't meant to be there, that someone must have mixed up our results, read them badly. *Our baby moves around a lot,* I wanted to say. *It's probably easy to think you see something that you don't.*

"We had a scan two weeks ago that suggested cleft lip and palate," I said aggressively, as if daring him to tell me that it was true.

"We are seeing a cleft lip and palate." He looked at us, his face simple, calm. It wasn't emotionless; it wasn't pitying. It was just...quiet. "There are some additional things we need to talk about." The world held its breath for us; the world let those moments be suspended in cavernous rooms that we could walk in and out of a thousand times. I think this is a kindness of the creation, that time is something we can feel in our bones, that it will, sometimes, obey our need for it to hold its breath.

And then the words. In no particular order, since I can't remember which he said first—anophthalmia, micrognathia, facial cleft. Pierre Robin sequence. Genetic counseling. Amniotic banding. "We will be following you very closely. You'll come in once a month for an ultrasound and then more frequently as we get closer to your due date."

Was I listening anymore? Did it matter how often we came in? The ultrasound monitor was on but not showing anything live, just a frozen frame of Jack's leg. "Can you be our ob-gyn? Can you deliver him?" I asked suddenly and without talking about it with Preston first.

Dr. D nodded slowly. "I can do that."

It felt like there could be nothing left to ask, even though I understood almost none of the words that Dr. D had used. After the anatomy scan, as OB-GYN offices call it, is usually when people start to really imagine the future: the colors of the nursery, the themes. It's when some people buy headbands or tiny plush baseball bats. Our scan wiped clean the canvas of our future. What could we possibly predict or imagine after this news?

My mind suddenly returned to the nurse's phone call. I had forgotten until then that she had also told me I should ask about Jackson's stomach. They hadn't been able to see it on the first ultrasound, which is not usually a cause for worry, but now the worry surged through me.

"Did you see the stomach on the ultrasound?" I asked, suddenly urgent. "Are all his organs there?"

Dr. D looked slightly perplexed. "Yes, everything is fine there." I exhaled loudly, but sucked in my breath again as I remembered the last, final question from the first phone call. "Um...and our nurse practitioner said my placenta is lying low?" Again, he looked surprised, a tinge of bemusement on his very calm face. "No, I'm not concerned about the placenta."

"So, can we have sex?" Words I have never asked anyone.

"Yes, I think you are fine to have sex." Preston and I looked at each other, trying to smile and not laugh, trying to understand how so much can change and stay the same in the span of five minutes.

We scheduled a tentative ultrasound date in June, and I was about to hoist myself off the table when he asked, almost as if he had forgotten, "I have to ask you this...do you want to talk about terminating the pregnancy?" He asked this quietly, and his eyes were kind. I think he knew it would be dismissed quickly. I shook my head violently, my teeth clenched. I had said okay in a smaller and smaller voice each time he used another word. Anophthalmia, micrognathia, facial cleft. Okay, okay, okay. But then he asked me if I wanted to talk about termination. It had been only minutes since we'd witnessed the parts that the tech called "Baby's"—Baby's heart, Baby's lungs, Baby's kidneys. The blood flowing from me to him, but his own heart beating it through the chambers, through the body. All these pieces of Jack we had just agonized over, thousands of pictures, and suddenly he would be gone if I said yes.

If I said yes, I want to terminate, Jack would disappear. Jack would not be here. How can that be?

It had been his body not forty minutes ago, and now it was mine, spare tissues I had built so I had a right to dispose of it, in light of the unexpected, the unforeseen, the difficult.

I said no. Preston told me months later that it wasn't just a no, not just a dismissal. He told me he had never heard that kind of defiance, that power, in my voice about anything else. I said no, shaking my head, my voice unable to form more than that word. I said no because there is nothing in the world that can change the truth of this: Jackson had been alive for so long, for so much longer than I had even known him to be there. Jackson was so alive, so joyfully alive—we watched even in that moment as he swam through the tiny home I had made for him, nestled in my skin, up close to my bones, his body stretching to feel the edges of me. I said no. We had named him Jackson; we had known his heartbeat and its separate melody; we had seen the plus sign light up in forty-five seconds instead of a full two minutes. We knew his life better than we knew most everything else.

But I have never forgotten that it was possible, even required, that someone offer me the option of ending my son's life, of eliminating his person, because of a diagnosis, because an eye didn't grow, because a chin measured small, because of a cleft in his lip and palate. How much that says about our inability to imagine lives even a little different from what we expect. How little it has ever said about Jackson.

★ ★ ★

After we met with Dr. D, we called the airline. We had tickets to fly to Boston to see my parents, but the urge to go home sooner set in as we passed the first few exits on the highway heading home from the ultrasound. We bought Panera on our way back. I asked for a tomato and mozzarella panini, but they had been discontinued a year before. I ate the two small substitute sandwiches they gave me, standing up in our kitchen, playing Page CXVI loudly, trying to drown the noise in my head with even louder praise and proclamation. I threw out most of the sandwiches and most of what I tried to eat the rest of the week. We wept and we knelt and we did our laundry and we flew home like birds who've sighted the first frost.

Our plane was routed through Dulles International Airport in Washington, DC. There, our connecting flight was delayed and we were put on one that wasn't leaving until the evening. That meant an extra set of hours to sit with this news between us like the unwelcome fourth traveler, the news that had latched on to Jack and would not let go. *Didn't they know?* I kept wondering. *Couldn't they see?* Our chaos was dressed in traveling clothes. Preston argued with the woman at the front desk. She put us on a standby flight. We walked up and down the hallways looking for lunch and sat down at a vaguely French restaurant. After a few bites of a dubious salade niçoise, Preston bought me a bagel at Dunkin' Donuts. I ate it sitting by a gate that wasn't ours. I paced the mostly empty corridors checking the standby list moment by moment. We were the only two who made it off the list and onto the flight. We landed and fell into my parents' arms, the silence cut by joy and the joy cut by grief.

That night we drove to my parents' house along Route 1, which snakes its way up the East Coast from Florida to Maine. Their house is next to that road, and for the first twenty-three years of my life it served as my own North Star set in the galaxy of my every day. Signs lit up every few feet of the drive, all familiar, humming distantly. There was the deathly rotary that frightens everyone not trained in Massachusetts driving. I saw the Revere Tanning Salon and its competitor across the street, Darque Tan, with its slanting black-and-white letters. And there, the warehouse-style gym. And then I spotted Budget Pools, the pagoda on top of the hill. And there was our exit, my former dentist's office, the bank, the grocery store, the consignment-turned-antiques store. I traced the outline of the thin elastic holding up my jeans, thinking of how I had once imagined telling Jack the things we were seeing. My mother chatted from the front seat, reporting on the weather and my two brothers' graduations, one from college, one from high school. Her talk just moved past me. There was the Dunkin' Donuts. There was the nail salon we never went to, the foreign used car dealership, and the blinking light that signals home. I named each landmark, each ordinary unchanged thing, my hand hovering over the one who had left nothing unchanged.

The next day, Sunday, we went to church with my parents. The building was a former Catholic church, the ceilings arched and swooping. Paint was flaking off from the years of wear and floated down as a reminder that the

Lord had long been worshipped here. I kept staring at
the stained glass high above the altar. Had a person been
up that high before, watching the space take shape from
above, a bird perched that much closer to the ear of God?
I wanted to climb up to those windows and see if it was
true, what I had learned all those years ago in medieval
history, that cathedrals are structured to draw us upward,
and hence, nearer. I needed to get Jack higher; I needed
to get him nearer to Jesus. I was the mat and the paralyzed
man on it. The hymns and praise songs sounded far away.
But I was climbing, climbing myself and my son up to
Jesus, the healer. My only thought was if I stayed here, in
church, still obedient, God would heal him. God would
see me and my son, held in suspension in my body, and
when he saw us in this posture of obedience, when he
saw us climbing, he would give us our miracle.

In the Middle Ages, people pilgrimaged thousands of
miles through Europe. Did people try to climb the buildings they came for, discontent like me with the ordinary
ground? Did they try to get closer, to stand on the top of
the duomo in Orvieto, when the sky was lit by stars and
uninterrupted? Did they shout and keep shouting, make
themselves heard by the God they loved? And I wonder
now why we don't know how they climbed the roof to
lower that man down. The climbing up with him, that
seems like all the work. We tell the story of lowering him

in to Jesus, but what of the ones who were climbing? What of the going upward?

The sermon was long. It rambled. I think the priest poured water into basins at the foot of the altar, but I don't remember what it demonstrated. It was the season after Easter, before Pentecost, the season where we proclaim the promises fulfilled, the deeds accomplished, the victories won. Surely it was here that God would announce one more victory, something small, for a girl and the mat of her body and the boy on it. Surely somewhere a woman hemorrhaging had touched the robe and gone away completely healed. Surely it was not too much for God, a small miracle, just the touch of the hem, here in this season of Easter?

I waited through the sermon, watching the stained glass Jesus high above the altar. There were two figures on either side of him: the lamb and the pelican. I had never noticed the pelican before, and I asked Preston later what it meant. He told me the pelican is a symbol of the love Jesus has for us, because a pelican will pluck out her own breast to feed her children. A pelican will become food for the ones she loves. And the lamb, the lamb of God, the lamb on the throne, the lamb is the sacrifice. Pure and spotless and undefiled and whose blood kept away the plague of death in the Passover and who defeated death itself. I couldn't look at the lamb, the victor—he hadn't won me a victory yet. So I looked at the pelican. *Please, please. If you are there, if you are up there, help me climb to you.*

When I prayed before Jack was born, I said the word *please* more than I had before in my life. I don't know why, if it was a hangover of politeness, if I believed that Jesus was more amenable to a request that began with an acknowledgment of the need to make the request a certain way. I said please, and *please* was the one word that could contain what I meant. It meant give my son back his eye; it meant give me the ability to breathe in this room with other moms whose pregnancies went the right way, with this blog whose mom got her miracle. It meant keep us safe in this car as we drive to campus; it meant where are you; it meant I hate and love you, that there is no God and there is always God. Later in the summer I would walk up the stairs in Morrison Hall at Baylor signing *please* in American sign language, over and over, my hand rubbing a circle over my heart. *Please* was my plea, my demand, my despair.

Please, please, Jesus, I prayed at the pelican that first weekend, its beak buried in its breast. My dress was tight, my shoes uncomfortable. I had earrings in, and the back of one fell off, in the parking lot probably, so it began to slip out of my ear. I wrenched it out and clenched it in my fist. The priest prayed for the whole state of Christ's church and the world. My family cried. Rachel, whom

I've known since I was born, the friend of yearly Christmas parties, who once taught me how to play *Frogger* on her PlayStation, sat behind me and silently tapped my back, handing me a tissue from her mother's purse. She didn't look at me as I took it, but touched my back with her hand as I turned around.

We took Communion in tears, and Deacon Martha let the cup linger beneath my wafer as I dipped it deeply, trying to soak Jesus in, imagining that the wine was a kind of medicine, that it would flow into my veins, a bit of that plucked pelican breast, and find its way to Jack. She looked at me, her eyes wide behind her glasses. "The blood of Christ, the cup of salvation," she said.

"Amen," I gasped, walking back to the pew with my head down.

When the service was over, Preston and I stood. Before we could escape the crowded row, Mother Susie turned to us. She was sitting with her husband, John; the bishop; and his wife, Sally, in the row ahead of us. Susie looked at me. "Hilary, would you like some prayer?"

She didn't ask what it was for.

I thought this was a premonition of the miracle, but now I think it was a miracle itself, handed to me simply, no wrapping paper, no hint or glint of the miraculous about it. I burst into tears and nodded, and she turned quietly to Sally. They joined hands, and Sally held my hand, and I clung to Preston, and there, in the pews, in the bustle of Sunday morning, they prayed over us. They named for Jesus the life inside me; they named it as precious; they asked for healing, for strength, for wisdom, and they returned to healing. At some point, the others in the row joined them, my parents, Father Ross. I shudder now to think how Jesus was not above but among us, how near he was, how the hem of his robe was brushing our feet as he, too, raised hands in prayer to God for Jack. How if I close my eyes, I almost write for you that I felt him breathe his prayers beside us. But I didn't feel that. I only wish I had, so I could tell you, so I could make it sound holier.

I remember the feeling of Susie's words in the air. I remember the downward tilt of her head, how Sally murmured over and over, *Yes, Jesus, please, Lord,* and how the men were silent, but I looked up once and saw that John and my dad were crying. I remember how Susie was wearing her priest's collar and how she looked so intent, her brow furrowed in concentration, her hands grasping those around her. I remember how the air was thick with our tears and how my nose kept dripping onto my hand, onto my too-tight dress.

I think now that the air was thick with holiness. I think now that the floor creaked with it. I think I believe now that Jesus did breathe his prayers next to us. He breathed them into Susie, and she breathed them out. I think I believe this now; I wish I had believed it then. I wonder if it would have made a difference, if I would have spent less time trying to climb the walls of the world as a way to Jesus. If I would have let him be as near me as I think now he was. But of course, I did look up. And there remained the pelican.

I hid in the bathroom to pray that night. The door has an old latch, the kind of iron or strong metal bar across that fits into a little notch, and a small flat piece that swings down to prevent it from being opened from the outside. It's a 1789 kind of lock, a reminder of the age of the house, of the lives and deaths it's seen. I locked the door and sat on the edge of the bathtub and I let the water run, which I hate doing, so no one could hear me cry. I sank onto the old rug in front of the tub, picking at the loops of rough cotton. I closed my eyes, imagined what a mother would pray, me and my running shorts with the string pulled out to make room for twenty weeks of child, barefoot, who couldn't feel less like a mother. What do mothers pray? What do they say to God about their sons?

I said that I hated God. I told Jesus if he could get up on a cross and die for the whole world, he could heal my son, and he hadn't, so to hell with it and him and the promises. I dug my nails into that old rug, stretching it in my hands, my knuckles white. If you love me, Jesus, if you love this baby, you will undo this. You will make this untrue. You will send us back to the ultrasound to hear that nothing is wrong, that it was a mistake, that Jack is fine, that we are fine, that I can go back into my world unchanged. You will make this a bad dream I've woken up from, a lesson of *almost* to keep me from worrying too much about whether he should sleep in a swing or whether I should wear him constantly or only in the mornings. If you love me, Jesus, you will make this like all those other *almosts* that you give your other children: I *thought* I would lose my job, my health, my child. I *almost* lost, I *almost* didn't have. And then you rescue them, set their feet back on the rock of you, give them back tenfold what you never took away to begin with, because the lesson can always be learned with an *almost*, Jesus.

I asked God to undo Jackson's diagnosis every day of my pregnancy. I asked God to undo that first phone call. I asked God to give us an *almost*.

I am giving you Jackson.

★ ★ ★

We came home from Boston awash in love and with what I wanted to believe was a renewed sense of hope. We had begun a new work of prayer long into the night on the two twin beds my mother had pushed together in my old room (the place where I had fallen in love with Preston, the place where I had first begun dreaming of a life with him, the place where I had stored a note in my iPhone of the names of future children—Jackson David being the first). We had felt the Spirit upon us at church; we had walked the campus of my high school, the place where we got married, with Jack wriggling in my belly and my new maternity dress billowing in the May breeze. We had begun to believe that we might be able to ask Jesus for something like healing. We had begun to say psalms and pray Compline: "Keep us, O Lord, as the apple of an eye," we prayed. "Hide us under the shadow of your wings." We went back to Waco intent on our hope.

But hope is hard won, and in the first weeks after Jack and Preston and I came home, I found myself sinking. I was reading philosophy for five hours a day in preparation for comprehensive exams, reprimanding myself constantly for the indulgences of long lunch breaks and early finishes. I settled into the familiar pattern of reprimand and resolution, and I wore this around me, a disguise, a cloak against what felt like the cold metal edges of the exam table that had become the world.

But of course I was not alone. I was wearing this pattern around Jackson too. I wonder now how often his kicking—insistent when I was at my most fearful, my most guilt ridden—was intentional. I watch Jack now fight my hold on him whenever I am impatient. If I am not singing with my whole heart, he kicks and paws at me, his restlessness marking my own. I wonder if he was doing this same thing then. I wonder if from the beginning he had been charged by God with the supreme work of catching my attention when I am at my least true, my least trusting.

We hung Jack's ultrasound pictures on the fridge, the pictures in three dimensions, blurred and difficult to read. I caught Preston more than a few times studying them intently, like a Chagall, a Rouault, asking God to show up in the shades of gray. I avoided the pictures, put my hand on my belly instead, asked God to show up in the feet and fists. We counted days and weeks and hours until the next ultrasound. We tried to live as if it was normal to have these longer appointments, to go *not* to the OB-GYN clinic on the third floor but to the antenatal testing unit, to the silent octagon-shaped room, to the place where no one spoke but you couldn't hear yourself think.

In the first months that we were home after Boston, I believed that God could heal Jackson; I didn't hope for it. The older brothers and sisters in this family of God chided me, positioned as they were in the icons and books we grasped around us. Martha of Bethany knew something about this. When she and Mary were mourning their brother's death, Martha's action, her feet, her movement toward Jesus, her loud accusation of his Lordship, this is belief that moves through belief, that moves to hope. Martha declared back to Jesus that "even now I know that God will give you whatever you ask of him." Martha demanded of Jesus the explanation, and her demand was filled with hope. She hoped that Jesus would live out an answer; she hoped that Jesus would show himself to be who she believed he was, who she knew he was. The Christ, the son of God. Martha put hope in Jesus, and her hope kept her walking toward him when he showed up late.

The Kingdom of heaven is like a mustard seed, Jesus said. Martha's faith seemed this way. When we meet her at one moment, the one we too often remember her for, she was concerned about the wrong things. Mary, her sister, chose the better way—she sat at Jesus's feet listening. Martha's faith then was smaller, less visible to us. Yet when she came to the road to meet Jesus even before he arrived at her house, then her faith was like the greatest of trees, wide and welcoming.

But I am no Martha. The weeks of June marched on; the weather got so warm that walking down by the river seemed like agony, the guilt at not exercising enough for Jackson the only thing getting me out the door and into the sunlight. I tried to pray a few times on those walks down the river, tracing what I believed with my feet along the concrete sidewalk, watching kayakers and ducks. I believed, but I had given up the hope that *even now* Jesus could do something for my son.

We all reach a point where we ask others for help in the work of prayer. It isn't popular in evangelical circles, the little I have experienced them, to describe one's life of prayer as lacking, as apathetic, as in need of assistance. We might ask others to pray for us, but it is prayer for something we need or want; it isn't to do prayer work on our behalf because our prayers have fallen apart. We rarely ask someone to pray because we cannot, to believe things for us when we cannot, to hope for things that we have long lost sight of. A friend of mine, Sharon, called me on a Thursday afternoon when Jack was about four months old. We had been talking for almost an hour when she asked me something no one had asked me before. "What do you know about God, Hilary?"

I was close to tears; I had been crying and not crying through most of the conversation. I had told her the truth—that Jesus was nowhere in sight, that we had lived into decision after decision where I had prayed for a protection I didn't think I had received, that Jack had not received, that it was four months into this wildly beautiful life and I was so weary of making it wildly beautiful for everyone when it was also desperately lonely. I had been telling her the truth: I had never felt so close to God as the nine months of carrying Jackson, and I had never felt so abandoned by God as the four months since bringing him into the world. "That he exists," I finally whispered.

"Can you say that God is love yet?"

"No, I don't think so."

"That's okay." She offered me a drink of water in the desert. It is okay not to know. But she offered more. "I will believe that God is love for you. I will pray to the God who I know is love for you. I will hope for you."

At some point we reach a moment when the prayers we need are not prayers *for* or prayers *about* but simply prayers, incense sent up when ours has already been spent. It is a dove or a pigeon sacrificed on the altar when we have nothing left to give up. At some point we come to this place, this strange and difficult place, where the need is not merely for someone to join us in prayer, but for someone to pray, period.

That June, and as far out into this life as we have gone, Martha was the woman standing before Jesus on my behalf, in whatever shadows of glory the faithful have as they await the final Resurrection. Martha stood before the throne, her arms stretched wide, and prayed when I could not, just as Sharon would pray in the mirrored months after Jack's birth. Martha prayed in our midst, her icon the only window I had to imagine how God heard his people. Martha, whose faith was at one moment a mustard seed, made a nest for me and Jackson in the great branches of her hope.

★ ★ ★

Jack was difficult to see on the ultrasounds because he moved so much. He dipped and swirled and kicked and hid his face almost all of the time. So, while a more common kind of testing in pregnancy is the amniocentesis, Jack was a rarer case, and our doctor wanted to see what the ultrasounds couldn't show.

We were scheduled for a fetal MRI for July 9. It was early in the morning, one of the first appointments. The idea was that the baby would be less active in the morning. I have never once seen Jackson obey these common ideas. He kicked and punched and spun around just as much as he always did. While I filled out paperwork in the quiet back building of the main hospital, an old episode of *Golden Girls* was playing. Preston watched, his eyes flicking back and forth to his phone, to me, to the TV. "I've never seen that show," I remarked after several minutes of waiting.

"We could watch it together," he offered, as he always does.

They called me back and I undressed in the bathroom of a medical version of a locker room. I slipped off my clothes and put on two hospital gowns, one like an apron, one like a coat. I waited there. A boy of probably sixteen or so waited there, too, turning the pages of an old gardening magazine. He had on loud yellow socks and looked like he knew how to have MRIs. I wanted to cry.

Why does anyone know how to have an MRI? Why does anyone have a look of expertise, of resignation, of certainty of what is to come in this place? I would come to ask these questions all the time as I watched people in the hospital. There is a luxury of being unfamiliar with the place, and however much I wished I could know my way around in the beginning, I now wish I didn't. I now wish we went to the hospital so rarely that we never looked at each other to silently divide the tasks. You bring the milk in the cooler; I have extra size 2 diapers in my bag; we will call the hotel; and we will go to Target when someone forgets to pack jeans.

This boy, his ears cased in headphones, flipping through an old magazine, shouldn't have to know how to do an MRI. The nurse who came back for him greeted him by name. "Hi, Daniel." They shuffled back to the room together. I missed his loud socks, and I wished I could see him again.

The radiologist herself came back to see me before

anything got started. I had never had an MRI before—
isn't it strange how many new experiences I undertook
for Jackson? This is a mystery of being pregnant. I was
always and never the patient, always and never under
scrutiny. I took on the work of testing so that, at least for
those nine short months, he didn't need to.

She explained that it would be thousands of pictures.
She explained that she would read them carefully and
write up a report. She explained that she trained for this
type of MRI specifically at the place where they basi-
cally invented it, a place where they specialize in fetal
surgery, interventions while the womb is still hiding the
baby from the world. I didn't feel much better but I did
follow the nurse a few minutes later down the hallway
and into the bright, white room.

They asked me to lie on my left side, the way I did to
sleep, and to keep remarkably still. The baby moved so
much it was even more important that I didn't move. I
settled into what I thought was a comfortable position.
They don't tell you that in the small cylinder you lose
track of time, that minutes suddenly are days and your
muscles begin to leach out their hatred of you. My left
leg gave up and just started to throb. My right leg, sym-
pathetic to my left, tried to levitate away from it. Sweat
poured from my hairline down my face and I was so
afraid to say anything that it was probably fifteen minutes

before I managed to squeak out, "My pillow is, um, soaked with sweat?"

The MRI took an hour. Like every ultrasound before it, they mentioned as it was progressing that, as usual, Jackson didn't keep still for the pictures of his face. He turned in toward my pelvis; he turned upward or outward. Thousands of pictures to assemble one idea of one face, one brain and heart (which, by the way, a fetal MRI can't help with much because the heart is a relentless muscle and never ceases its movement). But the MRI has a power that ultrasounds don't, peering in through my skin and muscle, and Jackson's own, and so the radiologist must have settled in sometime that week to read the scans. I went home and lay on the couch, feeling Jack kick in his usual exuberance.

Dr. D called the week of my birthday to explain the results to me. As usual, I was studying for comps, so I missed the phone call. When I heard his thirteen-second voice mail, I called him back right away—on a direct phone number I didn't remember to memorize for the future—and he picked up. "Has the radiologist called you?" he asked.

"No, not yet."

"Okay. Well I've read through her report and I'll walk you through the major points." I breathed. We had prayed, we had trusted, we had said to each other, day by day, "No news is good news," and, "We have no reason to think there will be anything else."

"The scans confirm some of the things we already know—there is a cleft lip and palate, no eye." A small pause.

I nodded, but of course he couldn't hear me nodding, so I said, "Okay."

He went on. "There is some slight narrowing of the airway, so the radiologist recorded it and is recommending that a nurse and doctor from the NICU be present for the delivery. It's not a bad prognosis, but this is a good precaution." Another small pause, another *okay*.

"There was something new."

I pressed the palm of my free hand hard against the cold granite of our kitchen island. Something new. Something more. He didn't wait for me to give him permission to speak, and as he began to explain, I found a pencil and the back of a credit card envelope and I started to write down what he was saying. "There seems to be some abnormality of the external ear on the right side. There is what appears to be an earlobe, but no external ear has formed. There is no ear canal that the radiologist could discern."

"Okay."

"The good news is that the internal structures of the ear are present, so there is a good chance he could hear out of that side eventually, through a surgery. A surgery could reconstruct an external ear."

"Okay."

"Do you have any questions?"

I think I asked him something about the brain, the heart, other organs. We went through the list again, familiar reassurances, and I said goodbye, thanking him for the phone call. Preston had been pacing by the couch, waiting for me to hang up. I took a breath, looked up at him, and started to talk. I tried to talk faster than my tears, to outrun the despair that offered itself to me, always at the ready, always the first and easiest thing to feel. Preston's eyes widened, and he held out his arms, and I fell into them. My husband has taught me more than anyone else about what it means to widen yourself for what is brought before you. More than anyone else, he has opened his arms and his heart and made room in himself for the wild, untamed, difficult, new. We held each other that night, not saying much.

A few days later, I wrote to my dear friend Agnes the news of the MRI: *MRI results came back—now it looks as though Jackson's right ear canal hasn't formed properly either, though the internal structures needed to hear are there. So there is another surgery needed to open that up. Everything else remains as it was—no right eye, clefting, etc. They still worry about breathing, as the airway is a little narrower than it should be because his chin is a little too small. There isn't much clarity right now about whether or how much this will affect his breath-*

ing. So pray that he comes out able to breathe on his own? Pray that we don't need a breathing tube or a feeding tube? Pray that we get to hold him?

I would forget all about these prayers, prayers built in the early moments, prayers about breathing. Above everything else, this was the prayer I asked others to pray for me. Pray that he can breathe on his own. Pray that I can hold him when he is born. Pray, pray, pray. The MRI revealed the last major diagnosis while Jack was inside me, and it was the precaution of the radiologist, her measurements precise against what must have been hundreds of blurred pictures of Jackson's two-pound self, that became the reason he breathed safely when he finally pressed into the world.

The MRI, which would be the bearer of yet one more mystery, one more missing piece of information, was also the reason that Jack had John, the respiratory therapist we most loved, present on his birthday. John's hands are immortalized in the first pictures of me holding my son, his purple-gloved hands giving him breath after breath. When we saw John for the first time in the NICU, I recognized his hands stretched over Jack as he twirled a sterile suction catheter.

This was our treasure hidden in a field: We did an MRI that let Jack breathe.

Chapter 3

WAITING

I began to hate Facebook around thirty weeks. I was weary of studying for comprehensive exams and found myself clicking on that small blue-and-white logo in my bookmarks bar more often. Just a peek into other lives rushing past, just a glance at the blog posts they're writing or the ordinary everyday Instagram photos that make me miss New England. That's what I told myself. Just a peek. It won't do any harm.

But I couldn't stop looking. Every day there was someone else who announced they were having or had just given birth to a baby, and for some reason, it was a summer of boys. A few moms I follow were sharing pictures of boys learning to walk and talk, small videos of baby babble and smushed cake at first birthdays. Other people were becoming moms, their bellies lit by glowing sunsets or bright afternoon photo shoots in fields, welcoming their pregnancies. I would sit and watch my feed, daring myself to click on the profiles of the people who already had baby boys or who were having them. I dared myself to be strong enough to look at the photos of a woman whose baby was due just two weeks after Jack.

The apps told me that Jack was opening his eyes—eyes, plural—and that he could hear from his ears—plural—around this time. The apps said play music; they said talk to the baby; they said do yoga to keep yourself limber for a natural birth. And these stories, from the other moms, they drifted farther and farther away from me, planning nurseries and debating cloth diapers and recommending pediatricians. Day after day, no music played through a special speaker pressed to my belly. Day after day, no yoga. I tried once and burst into tears as the woman talked about the wonder of natural birth, of quiet rooms and immediate bonding, and I tried to imagine it, me requesting a birthing bar in the cold bright lights of the hospital with the NICU team standing by. The photos of new babies, the animated graphics of the apps, they all had two eyes and two ears. *Isn't it amazing what babies can do?* they seemed to whisper, and I supplied the question—*What if he can't?*

Jack loves music, by the way. He sleeps to a looping

classical soundtrack on a small white music player in his crib. We walked in one day to the Pink Room of the NICU to find two different music players in his crib. "It calms him right down," the nurse for the day said. Jack loves to look at faces. A smile floods his face at the sight of me or Preston, at the sight of friendly nurses or people who laugh and smile. He smiles if you smile. He laughs, a tiny dolphin squeak over the trach, if you are laughing.

But I read these posts and liked these photos before I knew anything about Jack. All I knew, so I thought, was that God had taken from me the things I most wanted. It is selfish to admit, but I think pregnancy is a place of great revelation. I wanted Jack to be whole. But even more than that I wanted the uneventful miraculous birth, the birthing center setting, the cloth diapers. I wanted all my dreams back, and even as I prayed wildly for a healing that I knew God alone could do, I was also praying that God would restore to me the parts of pregnancy I believed I deserved. I was praying to have back in my life the expectation that people would flock to Jack, that I would nurse in the late hours of the night, that there would be no surgeries, no hospitals, no intervention. I was praying to get back a focus on nursery decorations and car seat models and how to lose the baby weight. I was praying for a back door of having all I had wanted when I got pregnant, which had so much to do with what I wanted to see in myself as a mother and so little to do with the one who had made me a mother.

Pregnancy is a place of great revelation, and I was revealed as selfish. I wanted everything to begin and end with joyfully expectant photos and lengthy discussions of which pediatrician, not which NICU hospital; which type of crib, not which plastic surgeon. I was desperate to be alongside other moms my age, desperate for the depth of conversation about kids when the challenges and questions got to be the same.

I cried about Facebook over lunch with a friend one afternoon in the library at Baylor. "Do you think, maybe, it would be a good idea to take a break from Facebook?" Her question was so simple and it was one I hadn't even considered. I stared at her, nodding slightly. "I just think," she continued, "it's a source of pain for you." I nodded more. I was at once embarrassed for the obvious truth of her statement and terrified of giving up my regular source of building the wall between me and "every other mom" I knew.

I wanted to be different, to be wallowing in my difference. I wanted the dreams to have died and the pregnancy to be anything but normal even as I wanted everything to be given back in a great sweeping miracle of healing. I wanted a story that was simple. Either all the dreams had died or none of them had. Either I was like everyone else or I was nothing like anyone else. I wanted a story where I was a consistent character with a consistent set of circumstances. I wanted a story where I knew what to feel, what to hope or not, what to believe or not.

I never did yoga or played classical music for Jack in the womb. But one night in the thirty-second or thirty-third week, it was late but neither Preston nor I was sleepy. We curled up on the couch with popcorn the way that Preston makes it best, drizzled with real butter and sea salt, and watched *Dreamgirls*. I had never seen it before, which shocked Preston, and we both cried when Jennifer Hudson sang. Jack kicked me during most of the songs, and as we got up to get ready for bed, I remarked, "Maybe he likes music." We laughed, and I put my hand over the right side of my belly, near my ribs, where he kicked most. "Good night, little one," I said.

Pregnancy is a place of great revelation: I was both unlike any other mom and united to all of them. I was different, and I was not.

★ ★ ★

"I don't know how you're doing philosophy right now— I would be a total wreck!" We were halfway through dripping ice cream sandwiches from one of Waco's most popular food trucks when the small group of women friends I'd met for dessert pronounced their surprise at my summer activity. I held a spoonful of broken snickerdoodle and vanilla ice cream in my hand, unsure of what to say. "Oh." I managed to smile half-heartedly. "Yeah, well, it's a lot to do, but that's okay." I didn't know these women very well, but I have a hard time making friends and I wanted to believe that I could make something happen by showing up to the gathering, by allowing myself to be seen. These were women who knew a bit about my department, with friends or spouses in the program, and had been around much longer. I sat there, waiting. One of the women continued. "You know you lose about eight percent of your brain capacity when you're pregnant." I swallowed, tried harder to smile, but I knew it looked like a grimace. I was wearing a peach-colored maternity shirt from Old Navy and maternity jean shorts my sister had sent me in a flat-rate box earlier that summer with clothes she had worn during her two pregnancies with my nephews. I would wear something she had lent me and feel stronger, more capable of being pregnant. My feet were sweating in those same floral sneakers I bought after we did the first ultrasound of Jack in Temple. I put my hand over my belly where Jack was sleeping, or perhaps he was listening closely, his limbs temporarily still.

"Well, if you fail them, they don't kick you out right

away. You go on probation first," one of the women said cheerfully as she finished her ice cream and set the Styrofoam bowl down on the table. I looked at her, trying to appear calm, trying to appear like I was laughing. "Well here is hoping I don't fail them!" I made my voice go up at the end of the sentence but the words caught in my throat and I decided the next best thing to do would be to pretend I needed to use the bathroom because no one would suspect that I was sitting in a stall blowing my nose with toilet paper, whispering over and over that it was going to be okay, and I didn't need to panic yet, and it wasn't wrong to try to take comps. I came out of the bathroom and made a joke about how often you have to pee while you're pregnant.

I'm not sure what it is that makes us press these worries on each other, back and forth and back and forth. Even before we knew that Jack would have complications at birth, I was asked how I would possibly do philosophy, do graduate school, and be a mom. I'm not sure if our imaginations are narrowed by fear or by custom or by both. I'm not sure it matters why they are, for the real work is to widen them again. The real work is to imagine what it must be like.

Carrying Jack while preparing for comps was in every way different and in no way different. I wore a lot of the same three breezy skirts when I had to make the trip to campus in the hot July sun to study with my cohort. I had more trouble concentrating after 3:00 p.m., and I was hungry all the time, which broke my concentration more than once. I cried when I read Thomas Aquinas on beatitude and Bonaventure on the journey of the pilgrim toward God, my heart a weary pilgrim. I sat at my in-laws' kitchen table on Saturday mornings with big compilations of Plato and thin volumes of Anselm and Scotus, and wrapped my bare feet around the edges of the wooden chairs. I lost myself in the swirl of ideas and found myself in them too.

I did philosophy because it is who I am, and I could not become Jack's mom by abandoning it. I could not spend the hours crying and folding his shrunken Gerber onesies without also lying on the couch, eyes closed, reciting to myself Seneca's account of anger. I did philosophy in the midst of waiting for my life to change because my life had already changed and philosophy was a silver thread running through it, a river I stepped in again and again to find it new every time. That's from Heraclitus, by the way, that phrase about the river. I read him the same week that we came back from Boston.

If I could ask anything of us, this ragged band of us looking for a way home, crossing the Jordan River, it would be to believe wider for each other. Believe for each other that God is gracious and that his callings are never in competition, that he who is author of time always makes enough of it. That when Jesus talked about worry, about the lilies of the field, he didn't have in mind that we would shrink our lives down to what was manageable, think only about number crunching or the next conference presentation or the kids' after-school music program or when she is old enough for a bike. He didn't have in mind that we would shy away from what looked hard, even impossible. I already felt like I was secretly cheating my child out of a good mother by sitting on the couch to rest, by doing philosophy every morning, by eating cheeseburgers instead of chia seed smoothies. I already felt like Jackson should have better than me. I needed the ones wandering beside me to believe for me that there was life in the vine for me, for Jack. I needed someone to believe I didn't need to be afraid.

The night I hid in the bathroom pretending to pee, after the gathering had broken up, Preston and I stayed at a hotel in downtown Waco. We were moving out of the studio apartment and into a small house in a different neighborhood. Our belongings were sealed in boxes, awaiting the moving truck in the early morning. I lay in bed, my heart pounding. I pulled *Aristotle: Selections* onto the bed with us and began to quiz myself, forcing a recitation of his metaphysics, the difference between essence and substance, the nature of the Prime Mover in

Book XII, where in the *Nicomachean Ethics* he discusses justice or the quasi virtue of shame. I became frantic as the minutes ticked by, my pen slashing at the pages of my notebook, my heart thumping. I was going to fail comprehensive exams. Those women were right. I had tried to do too much and look how far short I had fallen. My idea of studying seven hours a day had wilted under the hot summer mornings and the seventeen pounds I had gained. Who was I to think that God could still call me to do philosophy when I was expecting Jack, a baby with disabilities, a baby who might need help breathing? Who was I to think that God could call me to a motherhood that contained anything additional, anything like the life I had been living before that eighteen-week ultrasound?

The panic crescendoed, and, as it usually does, it crashed onto Preston as we lay in bed, Aristotle and Seneca and Aquinas littering the blankets. I had lost my ability to remember anything, and my brain capacity had diminished, and Jackson was going to have trouble breathing, and everything was so different, and these things came out in shouts of anger and frustration as my husband lay next to me, his head propped on his hand, his eyes wide and knowing. "You have got to talk to Jesus about this right now. Go on. Now." He got up out of bed and went to the bathroom and ran a shower. I closed my eyes, crying harder than before.

And Jesus came out to me on the water and said this, because this was a pregnancy of Jesus saying simple things, saying only this and nothing more: *It's just you and me and Jack during those exams, Hilary. It's just you and me and Jack.*

★ ★ ★

The week of the exams Jack weighed about five pounds, according to the ultrasound estimate. As the days drew closer, I drank iced coffee, a decaf version in deference to my doctors, from a Chemex that Preston left in the fridge for me. I took the exams with Jack sitting placidly on my lap, my chair pushed farther back from the computer than I normally like, typing furiously about gadflies and midwives and Socrates, about the political and contemplative lives, about happiness and virtue. Jack kicked and my legs grew sore from not being able to move them into my typical position, but as I wrote, I thought about the story I might someday tell about the summer I was pregnant with my first son. I thought about how I wanted to include Socrates, Seneca, happiness and virtue and the questions about air and water, fire and flux and change, about the foundation of all things and what it means to live well.

I thought as I typed faster and faster that the story of Jackson's first summer would be a story of philosophy, that searching out of wisdom. I thought about the days of the coffee shops and the later afternoon naps, the pondering with Preston as he drove me to Sonic for strawberry limeade and Tater Tots about what the differences were between the Stoics and the Epicureans, and how, I think, if one could be Christian and be Epicurean, I would want to be. It was a summer of philosophers, a summer of strangers on the new road toward God, toward motherhood. They were the voices that walked me through my final trimester, and they were the voices that offered me a promise that wisdom is worth seeking. Someday I would tell Jackson about how he sat on my lap in a computer lab at Baylor, all five pounds of him, while I chased down wisdom on a Thursday morning.

I don't know how I survived comprehensive exams, to answer that woman's question. I don't know if it was by praying or by avoiding prayer, if it was by panicking or praising, if it was the coffee Preston made me or the strawberry limeades or the hundreds of pages of notes. *It's just you and me and Jack, Hilary,* Jesus had said. *Just you, and me, and Jack.*

★ ★ ★

Jack was a stranger to me for a long time. He was inside me, unknown, his body a series of still lifes taped to our refrigerator. I didn't understand what was happening with him, and, truth be told, I was afraid. I was afraid of his face, of this tiny body now clouded with uncertainty. I was afraid others wouldn't love Jack, that we would be stared at in the grocery store, that kids would point and laugh or stare, ask their moms what happened to that baby, what's wrong with that baby? I imagined living my new mother days hiding my son from the world, resentful and frightened of what people would say, how they would behave.

I think I was mostly afraid that I wouldn't love him.

There is no automation in love—even the love most basic, the love flowing in that umbilical cord, the love breathed in and out, in and out again. It is not automatic that you love your child. It is choice and hormone and emotion. It is guttural and fever pitched and earth and sky. But it is not automatic and I was afraid that I would not love Jack.

I was afraid of my grief. I was afraid that grief equaled dismissal, that grieving Jack's diagnosis *was*, in the end, grieving him, wishing him other than he was, wishing us both in a different world with different faces and different paths and different everything. I was afraid that my grief proved, in the end, that Jack needed a different mother. One who was not afraid of disabilities. One about whom it could honestly be said that she took everything in stride, that she welcomed home any and all who were given to her. That wasn't me. I carried Jack in my belly those first eighteen weeks thinking he was something he wasn't, and upon learning more of who he was, I ached everywhere.

The ultrasound appointments were the worst. "But at least you get to see him so much more!" someone said to me along the way. I didn't say anything, but I nodded, hoping she wouldn't ask for more detail, the what-was-it-like. Because, truth be told, it was like seeing a dimly lit room with a tiny person squished inside it, kicking and squirming and hiding his face. I was afraid every time I lay on that table that we would see it, finally, and I wouldn't be able to imagine an easier version of it, an easier picture, a prettier baby. I was afraid this was the test of my motherhood and I would fail.

Before our July ultrasound I worried myself sick—literally, I threw up while lying on the table—before stopping to really look at Jackson. *Just don't make me look at his face. Just don't make me see him.*

But the screen was large and the expectations were normal, that me as the mother would want to see what's happening inside me, inside this home my body has carved out of my bones and muscles and tendons. So I looked up. His feet, his leg, the bones white and solid, and then, Jack's left side. The side where nature played the same symphony of cheekbone, skin, eye and eyelid, and nostril and ear, that spiral and shell. *I know you.*

The baby turned, pulling the placenta with him as he did. It perfectly hid the cleft, which we thought at the time took up much more of his face. Each time Dr. D wiggled the ultrasound wand, Jack hid. He peeked at us with his left eye, as if to see whether we were watching, though I knew he couldn't really know we were. But for one brief moment, we were locked in, his eye on mine (or so it seemed). And I realized, the tears creeping into my eyes—eyes, in the plural—*I know you.*

You are mine. You belong to me, and I accept you.

I think this work of acceptance was the most important work I did. It is the most important work I still do, daily, every morning and every evening, as the sun rises and sets, as I wait for the pieces of my life to reassemble themselves and as I admit, however briefly, that they never will again, that I must build with new pieces a new life. Every moment, I accept Jack. I tell him, you belong to me; you are mine; you are my beloved friend who teaches me that God must be gracious. You who testify to the Jesus I am working to believe in again, you are mine.

Love is strange, I wrote to Agnes in July. *Because I've been thinking that seeing him would be hard or scary, but the truth is, I didn't need to steel myself or brace myself or any of those strange metal-sounding images for seeing it. There he is, our son, our firstborn, playing hide-and-seek with my placenta and kicking me in the ribs and loving his life in there, from what we can tell. He is beautiful.*

When it was time for Jack to be born, I spent almost the whole time in labor with my hands on my belly. *You are mine, you belong to me, and I accept you.* Birth, whatever other miracle it is, is a miracle of acceptance. Whatever mystery it is, it is a mystery of belonging. "I know you, Jackson David," I whispered over and over through the contractions. *I know you; you are mine. You belong to me.* This is how I began to understand how love enters the room. Minute by minute of acceptance, of belonging, and of the one piercing eye of my son playing hide-and-seek with the placenta. This is how love enters every room I walk into now—with Jack, holding it before me.

Chapter 4

BIRTH

When we were about sixteen weeks pregnant, my nurse practitioner offered me the opportunity to do what the clinic called "centering." The hope was, I think, to provide a community for women going through pregnancy; through centering, you could schedule out all the appointments with a group of women due around the same time. We would go through the appointments together in an afternoon, she explained, and go through birthing classes, take a tour of the hospital where we would deliver, discuss how to care for the new baby, get resources for pediatricians, have a group baby shower at the end.

Preston and I talked about it. I thought it sounded okay—I liked the organization of twenty-four weeks of pregnancy listed out in neat fifteen-minute checkups, to-dos—but ultimately we decided to keep our original appointments. We would go to whatever birthing class could fit us in, I thought. My friends had gone to ones that were all day on Saturday or in the evenings. We'd make time and it could be fun.

But when we left that practice, came to Temple and Dr. D, and the category "high-risk pregnancy," there was no centering group for a hundred miles or more. I refused to consider birthing classes, which were never advertised to us anyway since we lived in the antenatal testing unit rather than the regular OB-GYN clinic. I refused to think about birth, about delivery, about breathing exercises or Lamaze or Bradley or tubs or birthing bars or balls or how I would like the delivery to go.

That May my sister and my best friend each delivered babies with grace and determination. I saw their pictures, the babies' surprised, glowing faces pressed against the warm skin of their mothers. They told me about the books that helped them, the natural breathing, the water. They told me about the strangeness and quickness of birth. I put books they recommended in my Amazon cart and deleted them. I looked up YouTube videos of the stages of labor and took notes in a Word document on my computer, but I never printed them out and I never made a plan. I asked Preston to make us a playlist of the songs we'd be listening to on our drives to and from Temple that we never actually played. I pretended we could still have the best kind of birth. I pretended there was such a thing, that it would at least be the gift I gave Jack. *You were born the right way,* I imagined saying to him. *That'll give you a head start.*

At our thirty-eight-week appointment, our doctor was in a delivery, so a resident came in to do my exam in his stead. She was overly confident and too nervous all at once, and I was at that point crossing my fingers that I had dilated more than before, since 1 centimeter isn't that much. I had been having Braxton Hicks contractions off and on for at least two weeks, and I thought, *Surely I'm closer. I'm almost ready?*

She told me that I was still about 50 percent effaced and 1 centimeter dilated. Jack was happy where he was and had no interest in an early arrival. As she swiveled back in her chair to note a few things on the chart, she asked us whether we'd like to go ahead and schedule the induction.

We stared at each other. Induction?

"I thought Dr. D said that we didn't need...I mean, we were going to talk about it and then decide...I mean, I don't think we want to do that..." I was flustered, visibly so, and Preston shifted his feet beside me and looked at me as if to ask whether I was going to be more forceful, stand up for myself and this baby, since it's my body, after all. Isn't that what they keep telling us?

"Well from what I understand, there are some complications with Baby, so I think this is a safety precaution."

My heart plummeted off the exam table, splattering on the clean tile. *Safety? Jack's safety is at risk?*

"Oh, okay, then."

Preston glared at the back of my head and I knew that he was skeptical of what this person was saying. (I would learn, time and time again, that doctors reading charts is not the same as doctors knowing a diagnosis, much less knowing a patient.) The doctor continued, and I kept my eyes away from Preston, the disappointment palpable. "Well, if you are going to induce, Dr. D likes to do that around thirty-nine weeks, and the spots fill up fast, so I think that you should go ahead and book a spot and you can always cancel it," she said quickly, smiling at me. I gulped and nodded, and nodded to a date and time I can't remember, maybe September 18? I was so afraid to say that I didn't want Jack to be induced, because it was about safety, and at this point hadn't I already lost so much that what would it be to give up one more thing, the idea that birth would be brought on by sex or spicy food or the simple readiness of the baby?

We left that appointment and fought hard in the car on the way home. "You gave up! You. Gave. UP. Hilary.

We don't want induction and we talked about it and you just left me high and dry in there, forcing me to be the only one asking questions, to make the decision for you. They need YOU to be the one to say what we want, what YOU want. You are his mother, Hilary. You gave up."

I didn't say much, just cried until we were at the Waco exit and Preston asked me what I'd like for lunch. "I don't know," I hiccupped. He bought me barbecue from our favorite place, the creamed corn I love so much, because marriage is that give and take, the ache, the love that builds it and bursts over it.

I called the doctor's office a few days later, left a long message that rambled about how we had thought about it and we did not want an induction, but thank you, can you please cancel the one you scheduled?

At our next appointment, Dr. D was kind, reassured me that it wasn't for safety, it was for convenience, and that he would let Jack be in there until forty weeks, five days. "That's how long I would feel comfortable letting you go," he said as he swirled the wand around to check position, heartbeat. "Everything looks good. He is in the right position." When we left that appointment, we both felt lifted, as though Jesus himself had kept Jack's birthday a secret, given us just a bit more time to pray, a bit more time for the miracle, a bit more time for the healing.

Because I did think about it that way. I thought that God had forty weeks, five days, to heal my son. I thought he had the time that Jack remained hidden in my womb, because I thought I was living in a story of revelation. That birth would be the unveiling of a masterpiece that no one could imagine. I told Preston I could see us with his parents, crying and hugging and singing the doxology while Jack nestled in my arms. I said that I believed I would breastfeed him, that my body would go into labor on its own, that knowing Jack, it would probably be right down to the wire of forty weeks, five days, because isn't that just like Jesus and Jack, to dream up that kind of miracle?

★ ★ ★

I wonder why I seized the idea of natural labor so tightly. I could not let it be. I could not release any of us—Preston, me, or Jack—from the frenzy of worrying even as I refused to plan. This mystified me. I had never wanted to give birth in a tub. The thought of me swimming in the waters of birth with my newborn child just wasn't something I could get my mind around, thanks anyway. I never wanted it until I couldn't have it.

When I couldn't do it anymore, then it was alluring and beautiful, a better mysterious connection to the miracle of a human being emerging from me. Then it was the only thing that seemed right to do, because it was more natural, because it was less medically laden, because it was—let's be honest—what others were doing and raving about. I never wanted or needed to have a tub birth until it wasn't mine to not want anymore, and then I couldn't stop thinking about how Jackson would probably be scarred for life because he was born with me lying on my back in a hospital bed in a gown instead of a bathing suit. I couldn't stop thinking about how he wouldn't be born into the hands of a midwife, how once you're in the hospital you give up control of your narrative, of the birth itself.

But of course when was it ever ours to control? I didn't think of that until much later.

I was great at paying lip service to the *all births are miracles* philosophy, which didn't keep the worry away. It didn't stop me lamenting and agonizing over Jack's birth. It's no one's fault that I thought this way. It is wired in me, to yearn after whatever is presented as better, especially when I can't have it. It is wired there by habit more than nature, a long tendency of longing. I have wanted to be the best at whatever it was I did, and in that moment it was delivery; it was preparation for Jack to come forth. And the closer it came, the more desperate I became to have what I could not have, to need what could not be provided, to give Jack everything anyone said made birth better, more miraculous. Did I think that a midwife would mean Jack was healed? Did I think a tub would bring forth a miracle when a hospital bed couldn't?

There was a different, difficult-to-explain grief that settled in me those last two weeks of pregnancy before we met Jack. We met the plastic surgeon ahead of time, to get acquainted, to learn about how things work in the cleft lip/palate team. As we sat in the clinic on the fifth floor—a floor that would become so familiar we wouldn't need directions by the time Jack was three months old—I was still wildly hoping that Jesus had a secret to reveal. *Everybody shall see the glory of the Lord,* that's what I sang to myself, to Jack, that's what I prayed, that's how I thought. When the surgeon came in, he started to give us the rundown of a typical cleft case: surgery for the lip around three months, surgery for the palate around nine months, followed by the annual checkups with the team, maybe tubes in the ears... We looked at each other. He doesn't know about the MRI. He doesn't know about the eye. He doesn't know about the ear.

I asked if he had read the file and he said he hadn't yet, that he hadn't had time. I was furious. Now I wonder if he had come from a five-hour surgery like the one he would do for Jack on a windy February morning. I wonder if he was preparing to split someone's skin wide and reshape it back into wholeness. Now I am amazed he spent time talking with us while Jack was still a mystery, when he couldn't get to know Jack's face by touch, tell where bone was small, missing, tell the size and shape of the unfinished work he would be asked to complete.

But at the time I was just angry. I didn't want to say the list out loud again. I didn't want one more moment of repeating what I hoped was no longer true: no eye, no external ear, smaller-than-normal chin; NICU team would be present at delivery; no anticipated breathing difficulties. If I named the list, it meant that he might really soon be born with all of these things. It meant one less chance to believe that we would have that surprisingly ordinary natural birth with natural labor and a tub on standby or a birthing ball and no NICU doctors in sight. If I said it all out loud, it meant it was real, and it was too late for the miracle, and soon it would be over.

We met Jack's speech pathologist, Joan, that same day. She gave us a special bottle to take home with us, sterilized and sealed. It has the kind of nipple designed for babies with a weak suck, something that cleft kids have a lot. I threw it in the back of the car. Of everything in pregnancy, breastfeeding was the thing I thought about most. It was something I had dreamt of since we found out I was pregnant. I dreamt of the late night dance, the 2:00 a.m. comfort. I read posts by women who breast-fed all their babies and believed in whenever-you-want-it nursing and indulging the baby in a kind of bonding impossible to achieve otherwise. I listened in on a world of, *But how could you bond any other way than skin to skin?* and *But of course it is so good for the baby's immune system; it's what God and nature intended.* I thought nursing would make me a mom. It would be the thing that set me apart from Preston, from grandparents, from everyone. I would be the one Jack wanted when he was hungry. I would meet the need most basic, the need most holy. We come into the world hungry and afraid and I would be his comfort.

Cleft kids aren't always able to nurse well. That was the first thing I looked up in April. They can't always generate the suction and pressure needed to nurse, so lots of cleft babies need that bottle Joan gave us, the one I threw in the back of our car.

Perhaps this was the shape of my grief then: a grief of no longer being free merely to wait on a miracle, a grief of needing to make preparations while praying at all hours of the night that they'd be unnecessary, that we would laugh them off, that we would someday tell Jack, once upon a time we thought you might need to be in the NICU; we thought you might need surgeries; we thought you wouldn't have an eye. Perhaps this is the grief that is rarely spoken: the grief of no longer having time to suspend in midair above your life, waiting on its unfolding. The grief of descending, again and again, into the thick incomprehensible earth of your life and still breathing. The grief of a bottle for a cleft baby and a prayer that you'll still be a mom on the other side.

★ ★ ★

"Jackson David, if you don't come out on your own, we are going to have to help you," Preston warned Jack repeatedly our last week of pregnancy. I had false starts almost daily. We timed contractions only for them to dissipate. I described tightening around my belly in a Whataburger drive-through, only to have it disappear within two hours, leaving us to wander toward bed as the days kept drawing to a close and Jack showed no interest in being born. I was sleeping in forty-five-minute stretches, and I made Preston download all seven Harry Potter audiobooks in order to have something to listen to as I was attempting to soothe myself to sleep at 2:00 a.m. I went for walks around the block listening to praise music and praying that Jesus would hurry up and show us his handiwork, that the effort of my body would be rewarded, the quid pro quo from God I'd been seeking all my life.

I remember the days that passed, the ones we especially

hoped would be Jack's birthday—September 24 or 25. Days mirroring the celebration of Christmas in December, when we had conceived Jack. I walked around in the thick heat, all reasoning abandoned, thinking that if only I managed to bring on labor exactly nine months after Jack was conceived, I would be given the miracle.

We weren't planning to start our family when we did. I write that and immediately worry that I should do more to qualify, clarify, explain. We had been open to children from the beginning, all six months of it before Jack, and we longed for children in a daydreaming way, where you close your eyes in your decidedly kid-empty apartment with glasses of red wine at the end of a long day studying and think, *Won't it be fun when we have kids?* We weren't planning to start our family. And then we went to the Christmas Eve service at HopePointe.

It was the 8:00 p.m. service. Preston was serving as a cupbearer, so he kissed me fiercely and left to get ready as soon as we walked in. I sat alone in our usual row on the left-hand side, toward the front, facing the musical instruments. The bishop's wife came to sit in front of me and she smiled. "You'll get used to this!" Preston was at the beginning of his ordination discernment, and we were imagining, I know, the future years of Christmas Eve with me in the pews and Preston at the pulpit.

But as I smoothed my skirt over my knees and tried to

think of something to pray, or do besides reread the program, another thought struck me. An image, not unlike the one I had of Jesus presenting Jackson to me, after we first learned he would have physical differences. It was an image of me, not too much older, lugging a car seat and being trailed into the same pew by several small children. They were varied in age but all clearly mine, and there was a realness to it, to their mysterious faces, to the car seat and the handing out of programs so everyone got to hold their own. I could almost feel the tight bun my hair would be pulled back in to prevent the youngest pulling on it incessantly.

We are supposed to make a baby tonight.

I don't know if it was the image, if God said something to me like, *Make a baby tonight, Hilary,* or if it's just me wishing there had been a clearer beginning to the story so that I could demand a different ending. But I know that I looked at Preston sitting next to Deacon Lisa on the stage, and we locked eyes for a second, and I knew he heard it too. When we went to the parking lot, we hugged each other close. "We're supposed to have sex tonight," he said. "I think God told me we are going to have a baby this time next year," I replied. And from that one night, there was Jackson.

And forty weeks later, I was walking around the Baptist church down the street for the third time in a day, trying to coax Jack out of me on September 24. It's perfect, I thought, just what God must want. A symmetry, nine months of mystery, a revelation to complete our annunciation. But the day of the twenty-fourth came, and went, and the twenty-fifth and twenty-sixth just the same.

It was Sunday, midday, when Preston posted on Facebook asking for prayers since, notwithstanding a sudden change of heart in our determined baby, we would be helping Jack into the world by induction the next day. We had been to church; we had sung "O, the Deep, Deep Love of Jesus" during Communion; we had prayed holding hands during the final words of the liturgy. I was starting to realize that I had to give up the idea that I could persuade my baby, could reason with him, could make him arrive on a day that was meaningful or a day that preserved something I wanted in my first experience giving birth. I unpacked and repacked the small red bag of clothes and miniature L'Occitane hand cream that a woman had given me at a shower. I waited, and we watched episodes from the first season of *The West Wing*.

That afternoon someone commented on Preston's Facebook post about Jack's induction. The sentiment was something like this: "I don't want to intrude, but you should know that waiting is better. Jack WILL come out on his own, and you shouldn't disturb him unnecessarily." Preston didn't tell me about it at first; he simply replied and reassured the person that this was a decision we had made with Jack's medical team, that induction was what was best for Jack. The person persisted. "I don't mean to make you angry. I am just offering my perspective as a parent, that it is really better for babies…" Eventually Preston told me, and I promptly lost it, shouting at the empty living room chair like someone was sitting in it. I cried, too, my belly tightening with each practice contraction.

This was my fear, come roaring to life. I wasn't making a good decision for my son. I was harming him by inducing. I was the one who said yes to induction so it was on me to know if it was right. But I didn't know Jack, and I didn't know my own body anymore, and I certainly didn't know the will of God. I didn't know anything, and as I sat on the floor, my legs sprawled out in front of me, I felt the weight of the next day sink onto my shoulders, my chest, and run down my spine like mud. I was being induced. I was going to be helped in labor by doctors and nurses and Pitocin, and they would break my water for me and nothing would belong to me anymore, and I would spend the day hooked up to a monitor and I'd never be able to tell Jack about the wonderful birth that I thought I would give him.

Jack needed every medical intervention present at his birth. I still panic at the thought that, had I insisted on a tub, he might have gotten water in his lungs and that first breath—the one he managed to take before needing help—might have been compromised. Jack needed the steady hands of John delivering breaths down his tiny throat and I needed my labor room nurse, who held my hand tight through each contraction and pressed on my shoulder and held my leg as I pushed, and brought me a heavy white blanket afterward and told me I could close my eyes for a moment while they stitched me whole again.

But there is more, because this is a story about God. Jack was born on September 28, 2015, the day before the feast of St. Michael and All Angels, a feast day for singing some of my favorite hymns, for thinking furiously on the multitudes God created who praise him in heaven, who protect and pray for us. Three years before, on the Feast of St. Michael and All Angels, I was confirmed in the Anglican church. That day I promised God that I belonged to him, I promised my heart and my life, I took on the promises my parents made at my baptism. I was marked and sealed as Christ's own, forever. And three years before Jack was born, I knelt before the bishop and he placed his hands on my forehead, and he prayed that I would hear a new anointing on me, that I would receive a refreshed spirit. I hung an old icon of St. Michael, given to me by my mentor from college, by the doorway of Jack's nursery a few weeks before he was born. It was the feast of St. Michael and All Angels.

"For he shall give his angels charge over thee, Jackson, to keep thee in all thy ways."

★ ★ ★

The night before we induced, I sat on the front porch alone. We had been living in the house for only a handful of weeks and I wasn't sure where to sit. There is a porch swing, some steps, a railing. I sat on the hard concrete steps, scuffing my feet on the step below me, scattering a few early leaves. It was quiet, a moon almost full. Preston was inside, his parents having just left for their hotel— they were staying in Temple in anticipation of the birth— and it was a rare moment of silence with me and my son.

And I prayed as I had never prayed before. This is it, I told Jesus. This is it; there is no more time to wait or hide or delay. If you haven't already healed him, you must do it tonight. We are getting up at five tomorrow morning, Jesus, and then it begins, and there is no more time to wait and pray in the waiting. I am having this baby, Jesus. I am having this baby you gave me and there is no more time to delay. But I believe you have already healed him. I believe Jack will come out breathing. I believe Jack will come out healed, a miracle to defy the teams. I believe that you have put each person in place in that room tomorrow, that you have hidden from us the great and mysterious work for the purpose of expanding your Kingdom, for the one nurse who does not yet believe to believe, for me to proclaim loud over my son that psalm we have been praying. Jesus, please, I know I have asked only this, thousands upon thousands of times, that I have nothing else to ask, but please. I believe you already did this, that it is accomplished, and in your name, Jesus, healing happens. It happened for that baby girl who was supposed to be stillborn and who is thriving now. It happened for the couple at church who were told their daughter would never make it to birth and she is alive and thriving. It happened for them, Jesus, because of you, because you are Jesus. I have seen you giving me Jackson and I have heard you calling out here on this water. Here I am, here I am, and I wish I wasn't but I am here because I believe you, finally, somehow, I believe you enough to come out here on this water, far from what I know. Jesus, show us your glory. Let me sing you a song of praise. Let me tell the doctors what you have done. Let me tell my son the story of his healing, the story of you.

If I sit on the porch too long now, months afterward, I start to remember this prayer. I start to remember the depth of belief I had in Jack's healing, despite everything.

I can feel the weight of it in my belly, how it was alive next to Jackson, belief as rich as the oxygen keeping both of us alive. I start to remember, and I have to leave the porch.

Jackson was born around 6:30 p.m., twelve hours after we arrived at the hospital, ten hours after my first dose of Pitocin, seven hours after I got some pain medicine through my IV, and forty-five minutes after I screamed that I needed to start pushing NOW. The doctors and I weren't ready, and truth be told Jack wasn't completely ready himself. But my body was doing something—which I suppose really does mean that I was doing something—and I could not control the urge to push. The pain was a unique kind, and there were monitors beeping and a woman swept in declaring that my doctor couldn't make it and I needed to have the baby, so she would help.

I panicked for probably thirty seconds. Dr. D knew Jack, knew him the way we knew him, those flickering 3-D pictures where Jack played hide-and-seek with the placenta over the right side of his face, hiding the cleft, hiding the missing eye. We actually never saw an ultrasound that included a clear view of his face during the forty weeks of our pregnancy. Dr. D understood who the baby was and why the NICU was there and that I wanted to hold him. In the flinging away from me everything I could read or imagine about birth, I had clung to one thing: I want to hold him. I had heard about skin to skin. I had heard that the baby needs to smell his or her mother as soon as possible. I had heard that this was the crucial time for bonding and there is nothing that can make up for the feeling of having your son or daughter placed in your arms. This doctor didn't know, this doctor whose face I couldn't register for more than ten seconds at a time because the contractions were close and fierce.

I still don't know her name, only her face, her calm and determined face, the quickness of her hands and the sharpness of her answer about needing to use the vacuum to help Jack come out. She was sure of herself, the way she put her bags of midwife and obstetrician equipment down, donned the mask, made herself at home in the pain and the screaming. I wish I knew her name, so I could name her for you, but I think it's more important for you to know her by this—she made herself at home in the chaos of my labor and Jack's birth, and she trusted me, which made me trust myself.

My nurse held my hand during each contraction and she used the spare thirty to sixty seconds between them to prep an entire delivery room. The NICU team filed in, stood discreetly to the side. They stood against the wall, at first a precaution, a prediction that would come true just a few minutes later. I never saw the NICU doctors. I can only remember the cool palm of the nurse's hand in my left one and Preston's warm hand in my right, his other hand on my leg. And I pushed. Later, the doctor would say that I was so strong, that I could have kept pushing if I had wanted to. But time is not endless when the baby needs to breathe, and I screamed and pushed and the doctor guided Jack free.

He squawked. It was quiet, an echo of the future noises he would make over his trach, noises that would make us cry because it wasn't a given that he would make those sounds. But that first moment, when I was heaving with the work of breathing in a rib cage that felt like it was collapsing with the efforts of labor, afraid to look up at the mirror in the ceiling at what I learned was "a lot" of blood, I heard him. *He is breathing.* My first thought. Preston had gone over to see him, threading his way through doctors and nurses and anonymous feet covered in thin blue booties. He was going to cut the umbilical cord but there were murmurs and noise, and I didn't hear Jack crying; there was no scream, no protest at being shoved into the bright, white world.

Preston came back around to his former position on the right side of my bed. I looked at him, my breathing the question. He shook his head, smiling and crying. "They're going to bring him over to you, though," he said, and his face had this strange look, a look of pride, a look of wonder, a grief and a joy that dazzled me as my blood pressure cuff lay abandoned next to me, tightening around nothing, measuring nothing.

Jack came into my arms for about five minutes, enough time for me to feel the weight of his tiny, perfect self, to look on the work God and I had done in secret for so many months. He was buried in blankets with little feet printed all over them, his head in a blue-and-pink cap, his left eye closed, his right socket covered by two flaps of skin. I touched his face while John's hands gave breath after breath through the makeshift intubation system, the one that relies on a person and not a machine to count the breaths, to deliver the oxygen.

They took Jack back to the NICU and Preston followed. I fell back into the bed under the heavy warm blankets and I closed my eyes. In the moments after a baby is born I think the world stops, even if briefly, for the mother in the bed or the tub or on the floor of her car. Because the body is still a body, and pain, that faithful and difficult friend, waits patiently to greet you two, three, even thirty minutes later. Under those blankets, my eyes closed, the world stopped. I had given birth to another human being. I had met Jackson David.

I remembered something as I lay there, already feeling the emptiness in my still-contracting belly. Preston hadn't just shaken his head when I asked my silent question. "No," he had said so softly it was hardly even spoken. "No, but he is so beautiful."

★ ★ ★

I don't remember much of the first few weeks after Jack was born. They bleed together. Mornings and nights aren't well measured by overhead lighting and the faulty water machine, the lactation room and the silence of pumping. I remember standing in the shower one morning feeling the alienness of my body, how my legs still shook under me as if they were not sure they could support me anymore, as if taking Jack from them had taken their purpose along with it. I remember the day Preston brought my diaper bag to the hotel and I put Jack's *Jesus Storybook Bible* in it, along with the bottles and the breast shields I took with me everywhere. For the first time I felt like a mother, walking around with a blue-and-white-striped spill-proof wipeable bag slung over my shoulder. I remember staring in horror at the blood still seeping through my jeans at the beginning. Other moms had warned me, but I hadn't paid much attention. It startled me to realize that I was still bearing the remnants of pregnancy in me, that my middle was shrinking but still round, softened by the work, exhausted by it. It startled me to realize that I was in fact having a normal postpartum experience.

What I missed was time. We got up each morning by 8:00 to get showered and dressed and force down cereal or granola bars, then to Starbucks, then to the hospital. They don't let you eat in the NICU, so we had to leave in order to eat lunch or dinner. I had to pump every few hours, and often what I wanted most was my bed. I wanted the same number of naps that Jack took in his tiny warmer among all his tiny companions. But it was selfish, I told myself, to need sleep or food when my baby was physically separated from me, when I had already failed to give him all those things that were so important.

I wish that I could say I walked through postpartum with some modicum of grace for myself, but the truth is I didn't. I was harder on myself than I have ever been. I was guilty for sleeping, for eating, a wild condemnation in my eyes that landed on anything my body did. I was tired from holding Jack with his tangle of cords, and tired of every moment spent not holding Jack. I couldn't sleep more than two or three hours at a time because milk supply is a demand business and the cheery lactation consultant told me on the phone, multiple times, to just keep at it—*you're giving him such a gift*. I wish I could say that I set healthy boundaries or saw myself realistically, but I went back to metaphysics two weeks after giving birth only to fall asleep on my notebook in the middle of class, my belly a strange blob keeping me company, my mind a wanderer seeking shelter in any kind of order, any kind of familiar life. I wish I could say so many things about who I was postpartum, that something in what I had been expecting and praying for Jack had come through.

But I crumbled in the days and weeks following his birth. I folded myself up like a tent and hid far away. I couldn't stand to be hugged by anyone but my mom and Preston, and then I would collapse, willing my body to mesh with theirs for a moment. When other people held Jack, I flung my heart again and again against the wailing wall, sure that he would never know my smell, my touch, my person as his mother. Sure that everyone else was what he really wanted, this tiny stranger I would die to spare. I crumbled each morning and gathered up whatever strength I scrounged from the corners of my heart and hauled myself to the hospital. I walked around with my pockets full of my old self, her expectations and her hopes, her disbelief, her criticism. I forgot that I had been pregnant. I forgot that I was Jack's mother, that the nine months were my preparation as well as his.

People said they didn't know how I was doing it. I didn't, either. There is no way of "doing" the NICU. You get up and you enter a world with no sense of time, no sense of place. You measure your day by the timing of rounds, whether the occupational therapist or speech pathologist will be by today, the three-hour shifts of hands-on: diaper changes, temperature, put in a feed. You sit in squeaking roller chairs; you bring in water bottles or sneak in granola bars; you hold your son. He sleeps a lot. You are afraid that he is afraid. You worry that it is hard enough to come into the world without lights, noises, alarms, and scope investigations of your airway. You are afraid that he does not understand, and he doesn't, but he probably accepts what you do not.

It was months later that I finally admitted what I lost, emptied my pockets of those crumpled bits of Hilary. Only in December, in the middle of the night on Christmas Eve, when the laundry room had filled—unbeknownst to us—with backed-up water from the garbage disposal because of a plumbing problem under the house, and I stepped innocently into a puddle of it with my new slippers from Target. Only then, leaning against the washing machine with my hands full of crib sheet, mattress cover, and pajamas covered in milk that had leaked out of Jack's feed line, did I admit it. I cried and cried and held the smooth white machine for support, and there, in the dead of the night, I was a mother in the absence of my pregnancy, in the finality of the birth, in my son who slept in the room twelve seconds away from me, whose laundry I was doing.

I wrote this in a letter to Agnes, some late night in the first weeks of Jack being home:

I forget sometimes that pregnancy happened—it seemed so eclipsed by NICU and my speeded-up recovery in an attempt to cope with being in the NICU. I am only now in a strange way realizing the hours I missed with him. I mourn them sometimes. I don't know if that's right. I want to insist that there is good hidden in what happened to us, that the care he received, the surgeries, our making big decisions, was a part of being his parent even when we were apart from him. But I miss the fact that his first weeks are so scattered, that I wasn't simply being with him, but always with him and yet without him. After forty weeks of being with him constantly, I do think that separation was really, really hard. So now he pulls my hair and I could cry for the goodness of it, and I let him sleep on me whenever he wants, and I think long and hard about those early days, how the grace of God is sometimes not knowing what it is that wasn't given to you until much later. I didn't know that one could simply sit around holding the baby those first weeks postpartum. I didn't know that one could let one's body still carry the evidence of pregnancy, still need the same things—sleep, food—and be able to rest and revel. I didn't know that recovery should take weeks, because you've spent forty weeks growing another person and now their aliveness is separated from yours but not by much—the umbilical cord lingers on them. It was grace that I didn't know, because otherwise how would I have fared? Jack's birth was miraculous, good, and right— they can't stay inside you forever; they must be born; they must begin in the world—but separating from him for any stretch of time was (still is) very, very hard. And physically I still bear all the marks of having had him with me in that way—stretched places of skin and the remnants of the brown line down my stomach (what is that called?), aversion to spicy foods (though I am back to liking Indian, which seems a warmer spice than Mexican), and of course nursing/pumping. All my muscles are oriented around Jack—holding him, rocking him, being with him. All my bones are rearranging back to fill the emptiness, the absence of him, though he is near. How would I remember that I was once pregnant if not by muscle and bone, the umbilical cord that lingered on Jack?

It was grace that I didn't know. I write that but even now I'm not sure it's the case. Was it grace or survival, or is grace the means of survival? I miss those nights still. I miss the weight I can't remember holding, his tiniest self, the bundle in the pink-and-blue cap and the blankets with feet printed on them. I miss all the times he cried in the middle of the night and I was seven minutes away not sleeping down the road, my heart beating frantically as I listened to Harry Potter audiobooks and tried not to cry too loudly. I miss everything draining and exhausting; I think on those hours of sleep I got and wish them gone, wish Jack back into my arms, wish the chance to change the narrative. That Christmas Eve, with the milk-soaked sheet, I felt for the first time like a woman who had been through birth, a woman who had given birth. A woman who had been birthed, too, into a new life on the other side.

Chapter 5

THE NICU

On Thursday of the week that Jackson was born, he had an exam by the ear, nose, throat (ENT) doctor. The exam involved a scope, which was moved up through the nose and then down into the airway, repeated going through the mouth. Preston had been with Jack all morning. I had slept in at the hotel, showered for the first time since Jack's delivery, my hair hanging down around my face like a wet sheet on the line. There are permanent kinks in my hair now from the NICU, from the season where all I could think to do was put it up in a bun, constantly wet, too tired to do anything else. When I got to the hospital, Deacon Lisa had just made it there too. I met her in the lobby, my diaper bag slung over my shoulder and my feet shuffling, since walking was still painful and I couldn't ease in or out of sitting positions without wincing. Lisa caught me up in a big hug, her eyes already full of tears. She had brought a little bear for Jackson. It was soft and I held it tight in my hand as we made our way up the South Tower elevators, to the third floor; had badges printed, showing our driver's licenses; and were buzzed through the doors.

Preston had gone back to the hotel by this point and he had warned me on the way that the ENT team was going to stop by "sometime" that day, not knowing exactly when. The NICU was run on the clocks of the busiest doctors, and the rest of us floated around them, our necks craned like herons to hear their words, their diagnoses. I walked into the Blue Room and there was my son, flat on his back, screaming at the top of his lungs.

His nurse caught me before the Purell had dried from my hands. He explained that they were trying to get a good look at his airway and he was "a little uncomfortable," and he was sorry they hadn't come sooner. Ryan, the nurse, to this day has one of the faces I'll never forget; it's imprinted on my brain from the time he instructed us in giving Jack his first bath, to his casual praise—"these parents are so good with him"—but I could see Jack turning red. Lisa and I went in and I put my bag down on the big rolling chair, the one they station by each crib so that parents can sit and have skin to skin with their babies. Jack hadn't cried like that before. He hadn't been that upset about anything before. I started to cry. Lisa started to cry, too, and then she asked me, "What do you want to say to Jesus right now?"

"I hate you for doing this to us," I gasped, and the tears raced each other down my cheeks and Jack screamed and the nurse came back, suggested with his hand on my arm that we wait in the parents' lounge for the ENT to finish, that Jack would be okay, that it would be okay. We followed his suggestion and went back to the parents' lounge, with the loud ice maker, the fridge we never used, the TV that was always tuned to Nickelodeon or reruns of *Everybody Loves Raymond*. Lisa asked me to talk to her, to tell her what was going on. What was there in the midst of that hatred, that anger with God?

I don't remember any of what I said. I just remember that she smelled like flowery body wash and her arms reminded me of my mother's, her hands broad enough to stroke my back, to make that motion a prayer. I remember that the room was strangely bright and dark at the same time and the couch was covered in graham cracker crumbs, the only snack they offered, and I think I ate one Kashi granola bar as I waited, hiccupping down the almonds.

The ENT team came back. Dr. P introduced himself,

shook my hand, and took a seat at the table. I stayed on the couch, leaning forward, trying to keep my heart from pounding too loudly. His team, the interns and residents, hovered like bees at a blocked entrance to the hive, unsure whether to sit or stand, whether to shake my hand or steer clear of the woman who had sobbed as hard as her baby during their exam. The doctor started with, "Well," and I think it was then that I knew I would not breathe until he had left.

"Well, I've just had a look at Jackson's airway, and I'm not going to lie to you, it's difficult."

This couldn't be happening. Jack had extubated himself only a day after he was born, grabbed the breathing tube and coughed like a champion, according to the early nurses who found him doing it, and the first time I saw him, really took him in, he had been breathing room air and lying on his right side, still hiding his cleft from me, his tiny dark eye glinting in the fluorescent morning light. His airway was maybe supposed to look a little narrow, but not be difficult. He had been breathing room air for almost a week. We had plans to try bottle-feeding; the hotel room had only been booked through next Wednesday.

The doctor continued. "The anatomy in his jaw just isn't there to support his tongue, keep it forward. He has a lot of trouble being on his back, and his tongue is obstructing his airway in that position, which is precarious. The anatomy is just...if he is in the wrong position, it can be a real problem."

I took a deep breath and as I leaned forward, he kept talking. "There is more. Jackson's septum has deviated, to the left, so it's blocking his left nostril. He can't breathe through that side—I couldn't even get my scope in that side. And"—*And?*—"he has a pretty severe case of laryngomalacia." (This sounded like "lair-in-jo-malasia.") I looked at him blankly. Should I know what that is? "His vocal cords are floppy, the cartilage is soft, and so I would say that his airway problems extend further than we thought originally." *When will he stop talking?* I thought. *When will he stop saying unpronounceable words that don't belong to us, or to Jack?* I kept looking at him, at the cracked leather of the couch imprinting itself slowly on my sweaty upper thighs. I could feel Deacon Lisa breathing next to me. The interns looked at each other, not out of concern for what was next, but in bewilderment, perhaps at the strange hum of the water filter and the ice machine, perhaps at the hum of the TV we couldn't turn off, the flicker beneath the closed door of the small bathroom. Above my head there were pictures from last Christmas, Santa with the NICU babies, testimony cut out with crescent shapes and fleur-de-lis in bright pink and blue and green paper, testimony that the NICU is precious, life changing, lifesaving, that Santa comes here too. But does Jesus?

"With a situation like this, the only solution I can think of is to put in a tracheostomy tube."

"Okay. I don't know what that is," I accused him. Using words I don't know about my baby isn't a solution, isn't enough.

"I would make a small incision in his neck and create a tunnel of tissue, and put in a trach tube, and then the air would bypass the anatomical problems and go in and out directly through his trachea."

"Okay. How long would he need this? He's supposed to get reconstructive surgeries."

"I couldn't say. He has a difficult airway, so while it might not be forever, I would say this would be a fairly long-term trach."

It was then that I must have started to cry, but I only noticed the tears when they hit my chin, the cold on my cheeks, how the room became hot and unbearable and the doctor in his scrubs swam before me, the scope still around his neck, his eyes protected behind plastic goggles like the ones I wore the two brief years I tried to play lacrosse in high school. "You can talk about it with your husband and then make a decision," he said, or something to that effect, and I thanked him and he left, the troop of students trudging behind him.

"He has a difficult airway, so while it might not be forever, I would say this would be a fairly long-term trach." I repeated these words to Lisa, looking at her for the denial, the prayer, the ushering in of the presence of Jesus, who could heal Jackson instantly, immediately, who surely could still pass us by.

"You're in shock right now, but it's going to be okay," she said, and she let me make a large round wet spot on her dark jeans as I put my head down and cried, and cried, and cried, the smiling pictures of Santa with babies and their tiny nasal cannulas keeping watch above me. Santa always remembers the NICU, but where was Jesus?

I called Preston, and he came into the NICU, the three of us violating the two-person-by-the-bedside-at-a-time rule. The nurse on night shift for Jackson started forward to protest, to correct us, but Ryan stopped her and explained, "They've just had hard news." I stood away from Jack's crib, afraid to go too close, to grow too close. Preston sat on the cold squeaky floor nodding, crying, and nodding. I looked over at Jack, the tiny teddy bear from Lisa tucked into his warmer, afraid and in love. We said okay a thousand times. It's tattooed on our ring fingers from our honeymoon when the word was our always, our fault in the stars, our fresh love. We said okay now, tattooing it on our hearts, on each other, on Jack. It is the one remnant of prayer that has remained. It flutters like a tattered, defiant flag on the edges of ourselves and our family. Okay, we said, we'll have a care conference; we'll take the next steps; we'll pray.

Jesus still has time to pass us by, I thought as we kissed Jack goodbye. *Jesus only needs to walk by once, and even Santa Claus seems to do that here.*

★ ★ ★

Our third week in the NICU, we had a conference with Jack's doctors in a broom closet, the tables and chairs difficult to navigate. By this point we felt like old hands at the hospital. We weren't asked to show our IDs anymore at the front desk; they knew we were Jackson's parents. We even reminded the workers sometimes that he was in the Pink Room, not the Blue. By this time Jack had a blue, yellow, and red crib, a more permanent fixture. The nurses cheered, something about how it meant he was such a big boy. The Pink Room was a long-term place. Many of the babies we saw there were working their way free of IVs, the plastic boxes giving way to warmers, to cribs, sometimes skipping one or the other in favor of the two hours of babe bundled into the now dusty car seat, monitors blinking the normalcy, the ability to go home. In the Pink Room, the brightly painted signs of each baby's name, in gender-appropriate patterns, were crinkly with age and sometimes the sticky tack keeping them on the wall gave way. I tried to memorize the names, to think of them as Jack's first friends, the little girls and boys hidden under blankets and wires. People kept coming; people kept going home. I couldn't keep their names in my mind.

The room was almost always dim. One little bundle after another, their names never clear to us, and the nurses couldn't tell us who these friends were, so you gather what you can, pray in half sentences, let Jesus fill in the names. The Pink Room was a keep-to-yourself place, or perhaps that was me. I remember after Jack got the trach, the "child life specialist" (I think she's a counselor; I wish she called herself that) came over and asked me if I'd like to scrapbook with the other NICU moms. I said no thank you. My eyes widened in panic, and, rushing, I asked her if the hospital taught American sign language (ASL). I asked if she could recommend a counselor in the Waco area.

The NICU moms scrapbooked in the room where the ENT had first told me my son had a difficult airway. They littered that table with pink and blue and green paper, with glitter and photos, with holiday stickers and labels— "My First Halloween" and "My First Thanksgiving"— and this is what I couldn't believe, that I was one of the NICU moms, that my son hadn't needed just a few days under bili lights, a few days of monitoring, some help with a difficult latch, some help opening his eyes. I couldn't believe that I was one of the long-term moms who lived in a rhythm of hospital elevators and stealing the breast pump from one NICU room to the other. I couldn't believe that I was being invited to record the fact that his first Halloween (the holiday for tiny pumpkin costumes, the holiday for pirates) hadn't been at home.

So I asked about ASL and counseling. The child life specialist looked at me, astonished, happy maybe, also probably a little sad. I was so determined to reject what I know now was kindness and help. I was so determined to not need her or the pinking shears or the holiday stickers, to tell a story where maybe no one would notice our six weeks in the ark of the South Tower. Maybe no one would notice that our world had collapsed into two chairs pulled up by a crib, that we ate Whataburger multiple times a week because there wasn't much else in Temple and I needed calories for pumping, that we drove back to Waco only for my lonely, weekly metaphysics class where we debated the nature of persons and free will.

This is the ark we crowded ourselves onto, pushed in with our ghosts and dreams, our long drives that summer where we had imagined we would never be in the hospital more than two days. We stopped wearing our wedding rings and started wearing Purell. We went to Target and bought a mobile, gray and white, Noah's ark themed, giraffe and zebra and lamb twirling around. We had to unscrew it whenever we did trach care on Jack, and I grew to hate it, that cheerful symbol of our moving in, making ourselves comfortable. We never played it for Jack, and I don't know if he ever looked at it, but it hovered over him, a ghost of home. Every time we washed our hands, we did it outside the room, like surgeons do outside the OR. Perhaps we were surgeons operating on our own hearts, our past selves, scalpeling away what had become dead weight, freeing ourselves and our son from all that we had thought life would be, to make room for what must be.

The Pink Room was quiet, eight beds total, and Jack had slot 42, by the window that overlooked the back parking lot of the hospital. He grew there for two weeks—which now sounds so brief, a fortnight, a slip of days—before all the specialists could find a time to be together.

It was seven in the morning. Jack was asleep, and we had snuck in coffee in smooth white Starbucks cups, and I was wearing my black shirt with swans printed on it, slippery against my skin. The specialists were bright, almost too bright, in that small room around a too-big table, the table where we had first met a NICU doctor, the table where we would learn CPR specifically for infants with trachs. The plastic surgeon asked me if I could summarize what I understood about Jackson's condition. My voice came out in lumps, a sentence or two at a time, and I clung to the medical language, parroting the morning briefings we overheard often. I made them a list, like the ones we'd heard so many times before. *Sleep apnea, airway blockage, lair-in-jo-malasia, missing upper mandible.* Preston nodded and swiveled in the chair next to me. I finished and it was quiet. "Yes, that's very well put," the neonatologist finally said.

We had come prepared to do battle over the trach. We had come prepared to talk these doctors down off the ledges of *only way to thrive.* We are theologians, poets, and philosophers. We are parents, and we came in with those banners folded in our pockets to whip out in front of them. Preston only said one thing, though, the whole time, and I fell silent, knitting my fingers together and unlacing them in my lap. Preston told them they needed to be sure it was right, that there was nothing that could be done, that we could get a second opinion, you know—he said these things, and they fell softly to the floor beside us as the doctors looked at each other, at us.

There was compassion, I think, not pity. There was understanding, too, more of it in that room of doctors, in that room I hated, than in most of the rooms I enter now.

I listened as they made us a new list, a list about development, thriving, grabbing toys, gaining weight, staying free of illness all winter, a list of hope in tiny silicone tubes, in what we as parents could learn about Jack, what we could do for him, what we could give him. As I listened, I felt myself suddenly past the point of decision. Jackson would get the trach. Jackson needed it; it was done, and I was descending, fast and hard, into the depths of it, driven by their kindness, by their certainty, by God.

It was the trach nurse's words, I think, that must have been the moment I knew where I was, what we were doing. She looked at us in her dark blue scrubs, her name badge with the bold RN label above it, silver earrings dangling from her ears. "Your son, he doesn't know how easy breathing is. Right now, it's work for him, and it can be so easy, and with a trach, it will be."

The doctors filed out, and our social worker gave us "all the time we needed" in the room alone, the door closed. Another doctor—with another family, I wonder?—started to open the door but the social worker moved them away. It took us only a few minutes to speak.

"He needs the trach," Preston began. "I think we know what we are doing."

I nodded. "Isn't this the point, in the end? We want to make it easy for him, and do the work for him, and that's possible with the trach. We can take the work of breathing away and give him the gift of breathing easy. We can do that work for Jack."

We had come prepared to do battle at all costs against the trach, against the tide that lapped at our feet those first three weeks, against the difficult airway and the night nursing, the emergency trach bag, the possibility of danger, the pulling over on the side of the road to suction him. We had come prepared to fight against all of this, and we left holding hands, our arms widening to embrace it.

Isn't it strange, love? Isn't it somehow, in its depths, also glorious?

★ ★ ★

When I close my eyes now, I can map the hospital in my mind. I can build it, brick by brick. I walk down the hallway connecting North and South Towers, where the outside is cloaked in tarps from construction. I make a sharp right by the self-playing piano, which plays old jazz numbers. The silent slate-blue linoleum gives way to less comfortable teal and red and tan chairs in zigzag and check patterns. If I keep going straight, eventually I find my way to a hidden waiting room for a clinic I never see the sign for, faces waiting or mourning, rejoicing or resting. I go past a registration desk where they ask for blood donors every day, all the way to the cafeteria and the small Subway where once my mom bought me two sandwiches, which I plowed through, and two bags of Sun Chips and four cookies and a large soda. That was when I didn't understand my body or what it needed. I mistook hunger for sadness, and anger for hunger. I ate at strange times those six weeks, hours that never seemed right to eat in before, but to this day at three in the morning I want Oreos, Sun Chips, and Coke.

There are snaking hallways that go to the clinic where Preston and I first met Dr. D and had our confirmation ultrasound. If I walk long enough, I come out the other end of the clinic part of the hospital, onto a dirty concrete sidewalk, and I can walk loops up and down looking at a parking lot on my left and a sea of other buildings on my right, all the same gray-brown, that housed other specialized clinics: rehabilitative medicine, a pharmacy. The hospital in Temple spreads its wings over the town, casts bits of buildings off down other streets so that, just when you think you've left it behind, you see the cheerful green-and-white logo, naming another kind of thing you need a doctor for, and you realize you've never left. Perhaps you never can.

If I take the South Tower elevators up to the third floor, I am deposited in front of the OB registration desk. It's surprisingly small, only a handful of chairs, as if they expect that everyone who comes with a woman who is in labor will want to stand at the ready, will want to pace. They give you a clipboard, a stack of forms, ask you to wait for the triage nurse. I went three times in my life. Once it was a false alarm about water breaking, a frantic scurrying drive to Temple at thirty-seven weeks only to hear the steady, 130 beats per minute blipping across the screen. When I close my eyes, I can see the room, the pale scrub-blue jersey sheet stretched over the gurney, the way my belly pressed back against my chest when I lay down, the pink monitor stretched wide like a gaping mouth over my protruding belly button. I remember residents taking care of us, how we waited an hour because they couldn't find someone to sign off saying I could go home, that I wasn't in labor, that Jack wasn't in distress.

The second time we went up those elevators to the desk was when I was going to be induced. I picked a fight with Preston while I filled out paperwork at 6:40 a.m. I shuffled my feet incessantly and held the red-and-pink-paisley hospital bag so tightly it streaked my hand red with sweat and worry. I remember that I never looked to my left when I exited those elevators before Jack was born. Left was the waiting room. Left was where people held big parties with blue and pink balloons with baby elephants and monkeys on them; left was where people went home. And left, then right, then left again—that's where we lived. We waited in that waiting room for Jack's trach surgery. I never looked left before he was born.

But I can only walk left now, because right is an ended story, a chapter closed. Right, the OB desk, the registration, the triage nurse, the friendly IV specialist offering my Pitocin drip like it's candy...that way is buried far under the rubble of the first time we turned left.

So we turn left, you and I, reader, and we walk up to another desk, to a nurse, whose face we will always remember better than her name, her face thin and her glasses large around her brown eyes. She calls me by name—Jackson's mom—and prints my ID badge without asking for my driver's license. Then she presses a button and the door opens. We walk into a surprising brightness. The floor is white linoleum; the walls are a friendly green, blue, and purple, the colors of eggplants and our idea of grass and twilight, the colors of the children's hospital, because the NICU is an outpost of what is now our other home, our other family. We walk down this hallway, and if we duck right, we pass a storage closet whose door is covered with paper from the inside, and on the outside there are swirls of black, orange, and yellow paint, curlicues, bumblebees, I thought once, or Halloween decorations. Just beyond that is the parents' lounge; the humming sound is the water filter. There is one bathroom in there, which is where I hide from myself, where I bleed into my jeans and try to blot it with toilet paper. This bathroom is where I put on a dress for a date in Austin with Preston after Jack's surgery, when he was sleeping so much from the anesthesia, his trach so new we couldn't yet touch him. The mirror is angled off the wall, downward, pointing my gaze to my navel, to my toes. The door locks, I think, but I'm never perfectly sure.

But eventually I keep walking. I have to keep walking, because Jack is down the hallway. I might say it's fifty-seven steps to Blue and seventy-three to Pink but I never counted steps; I counted the sinks outside each room where you strip off your jewelry and scrub your hands free of the outside world. I never counted steps; I counted doors, doctors, breast pumps, and privacy screens. There are two breast pumps in Blue and often none in Pink. There are two screens in Pink, four in Blue. There are never enough of the comfortable chairs. Once while Jack slept, I gave my comfy chair to a woman who needed to pump, who couldn't hold her baby for all the IVs, the medicines, the drip, drip of worry and the hushed voices of the nurses who kept putting on new purple gloves and turning off her alarm. I offered the woman the comfortable chair because I could not save her baby and I could not save my own. And what cruelty, to sit so close to what you cannot save.

There are twelve beds in Blue, maybe more or less as the seasons change, but that's what I remember, and it's the brightest there because it's where all babies go before it's understood what they need, who can help them, who can keep them safest. There are some sinks where I rinse out bottles, but I never have energy to scrub them clean. There are two trash cans, one for linens, one for trash. The blue liners tell you the can is for linens. The cribs and warmers often have fleece blankets over them, the kind that have fringe where someone has cut strips and tied two kinds of fleece together, making the blanket reversible. My friend Amanda once made me such a blanket for Christmas over fifteen years ago. It was olive green on one side and cream colored with little bears on the other. It's on my old bed at my parents' house now. I slept under it when we went back to Boston. Here, the babies sleep in the shade of these blankets, these tiny flags of love, the proof that they are not forgotten. I bring Jack a blanket after a week, after I cannot bear his white too-big T-shirt and flannel blankets with the tiny feet. They tell me to bring things from home, make myself comfortable. We bring things in bits and pieces, always hoping we don't need to bring too much, always saying how hard it will be to take it all home.

But this is where I stop. This is the maze I walk, these hallways, these lights, these walls without clocks, these doors that lock when they shut behind you. This is where I am still walking, where I have never stopped walking. You go home from the NICU and you never go home, because your muscles build memories and hold them for you. My legs are still walking these hallways, my heart trailing behind, suggesting listlessly, quietly, that if we turn right, instead of left, if we take the elevator down, not up, if we drive back up 35, we might pretend it never happened.

Chapter 6

BREAKING UP WITH GOD

Jack was treated for granulation tissue a few weeks into being home. Granulation tissue is a vascular tissue, full of tiny blood vessels that can grow on almost any wound in the body. It is an overzealous, healing tissue, our body's way of shouting that there is a gap to close, a bridge of skin to make, something to repair. It's a beautiful thing, this gift of Jack's body to him, but it's not a gift we can accept now: The stoma in his throat and at his G-button site are meant to be there, meant to remain open, and so we grow used to swabs with silvernitrate tips, reprimanding the tissue back into submission. We had first noticed the granulation when changing his trach tube became more difficult, the small bubble of new cells blocking the entrance to his trachea. We went to the trach/vent clinic, where they swabbed the tissue with silver nitrate, and we went on our way back home. We promised to keep an eye on it, to call them back if we thought Jack needed to be seen again.

We fought to get insurance approval for a Mepilex Silver bandage, as opposed to the two-by-two split gauze the medical supply company keeps sending us in droves. The Mepilex Silver has a bit of silver in the bandage itself, so it keeps taming the granulation tissue and prevents bacteria from growing out of control. We reported to each other, compared notes, every time we changed the dressing or the tie or the trach itself. In the weeks after as we monitored the stoma, I couldn't stop thinking how strange it was to be fighting Jackson's body. We aren't meant to have silicone tubes in our throats. We aren't meant to have tubes that go into our stomachs, and the body tells us this, insists on it, fighting back by trying to close it. They often told us at the hospital to be careful when handling these wounds because the body is so eager to close them. He'll have scars fairly quickly, they told us; it'll look like he has a second belly button. This will close on its own someday. It isn't meant to remain open.

I didn't know before having Jack that the most complicated, hardest things are so rarely the things people think. We are all so used to the big news: a sick heart or kidneys or lungs, the need for a surgical repair, the need for a transplant. We so rarely talk about the things that accompany these big things: remembering how to space medicines in four- or six-hour increments, calling three pharmacies when a prescription goes missing, buying triple antibiotic the way that most people buy milk. It's holding your kid down on his changing mat while he rolls and squirms and yells at you, turning red, so that you can change his trach tie—the small foam and the Velcro that keeps him breathing, that keeps him unafraid enough to be yelling at you in the first place. It's being looked at strangely by a pharmacist when you request sterile cotton tip applicators, because surely, aren't Q-tips enough? When your husband explains that it's for tracheostomy and G-button care, the pharmacist is shocked and silenced, but the pharmacy doesn't have any anyway, so you call your supply company again.

And there are so many things Jack's body doesn't teach me: the work of parents who give injections or manage IVs, who hold down seizing limbs, who hear the steady stream of extra oxygen slipping into a nose or a trach. I don't know the work and labor of supplementing feedings for weight gain or sleeping for weeks at the hospital while they search for an answer to pain, to headaches, to nausea. I don't know the work of extensive genetic testing with an eye for a cure.

117

This is a major reason that I thrash out when people tell me they knew someone who had a cleft lip, had a heart procedure, had a mild brief surgery to have tonsils removed. This is why I sit in the stiff chair of Jack's surgical prep room in the third hour since he's been under and wish that I could hug the parents of the little boy who is riding a scooter in a hospital gown around and around while he waits for the OR to be emptied of our story, prepped for his. I want to grab him as he races by, tell him that I don't know how he feels, how his mom and dad feel, but could I just tell you, you are so good at riding that scooter? Someday I hope my son can race you.

It was so easy to know only the big things about medical technology before Jack. It was easy to know that a trach tube was something to help someone breathe. It was easy to know that ventilators did what our lungs do without knowing exactly what that was, easy to not think beyond the first word.

And then Jack got a trach and got granulation tissue and we discovered that it is always about what is beyond that first word, the spare trach bag made of a repurposed diaper bag, the amount of suctioning you need to do on any given day, the fact that if you're not careful, you'll spill half of a feed out of the med line in a Mic-Key extender when the stopper isn't in all the way. The weekly tube change, how to sterilize things at home in the

Medela quick-clean steamer bags, the fact that Mepilex Silver stains clothes permanently.

What makes it hard is not the fact that Jack has a trach. It's everything else that we never knew existed.

★　★　★

We learned about emergencies on our last day in the hospital. Our trach nurse breezed in on her way to another part of the hospital—CICU, ICU—and said everything briskly, almost an afterthought. "Of course you will go through these steps, see if he needs a tube change, evaluate his airway." Her clipped accent followed us around Jack's crib where we were wrestling him into his going-home outfit, a tiny orange vest and a gray onesie with blue foxes on it. We spent most of the time she was there evaluating the lingering stitch from his initial tracheostomy surgery, and she got Carly, his nurse for the day, to help her remove it with a suture kit retrieved from a closet somewhere in the maze of hallways. After that, it was only a packet of reminders, giving back the black plush baby doll on which we had practiced tube changes, and loading our car. I thought at the time that we drove home we would never need the packet, the bare bones of emergency procedures, our intuitions and hands that were steady around silicone tubes and open wounds. I thought God would at least give us that small relief, a certainty that while he hadn't given us healing, and he hadn't passed by the crib, he wouldn't let Jack die in our arms.

He has not.

I was tempted to add *yet*. What does that say about me, that I almost told you I think it's possible God would let my baby die in my home? But I am racing ahead, because there is a reason for the *yet*.

It was January, just a few months into Jack being home. Our friends and their daughter were visiting from Belgium, and friends in Waco were over for an Indian food feast. Preston was in the kitchen making pakoras and the nurse was with Jack, changing his diaper before putting him back to bed. I had gone into our bedroom to pump, the door slightly open. It wasn't meant to be, the point of being in the bedroom was privacy, but there was a wind in that door, I think. I heard a strange cough about five or six minutes into pumping, just when the pump switches from its "letdown phase" to the regular expression. I shrugged it off at first, thinking it must be one of our guests, perhaps our friends' daughter. But the cough continued. *The nurse is there; nothing can be wrong,* I thought, but my heart had quickened and I inched forward in the chair, ready to rise up out of it. The cough, again, and this time something was wrong; my heart was beating too fast for there not to be a problem. And then I saw the nurse poke her head out of Jack's door. "Can you help me?" she asked.

I wrenched the pump off and left it, helplessly sucking in air and dripping milk on the floor. I ran across the hallway and there was my son, his tiny eleven-pound self coughing and sputtering, his neck bright red and gurgling with blood. "He pulled his trach out," the nurse tried to explain. "I was changing his tie—" I held up my hand and I looked at my son, who had tears in his eye, who was turning pale, and I felt all the blood leave my body. *Get the smaller trach, Hilary. Get the smaller trach now.* I walked over to the bin where we keep his trach equipment, found the smaller one, put it in, and pulled out the obturator (the small curved bit of plastic that helps the tube keep its shape as it enters the stoma), and Jack took a shuddering breath. I stood there, holding the tube in place in his neck, watching as the inside of it turned pink from the blood. "I'm going to get Preston and we will do a trach change," I said, and the nurse nodded, her eyes wide and afraid, not just at what happened, but at my voice, my command. "Don't move," I said. "I'm going to get him now."

I walked through our dining room, which has French doors that open onto the living room, where our friends were gathered. Later they would tell us that they didn't realize anything was wrong, that Preston and I were "so calm" in emergencies, and I would hate them for it, for a moment. I walked into the kitchen, where Preston had his back to me, humming as he rolled spinach and chickpea flour. "I need you right now."

He followed me without a word, his face set firm. I explained as we walked into the nursery, and there was Jack, still in his nurse's arms, still taking those shuddering breaths and gurgling blood. "Okay, buddy, we are going to do a trach change," Preston told him, and we prepped everything the way we used to in the NICU. I took my position, ready to pull out the small trach and put in the new. But when I pulled it out, Jack panicked again, sure he couldn't breathe, sure he couldn't be safe, his eye looking at me full of fear, and as he cried, the granulation tissue bobbed up and down, and I couldn't see the opening; I couldn't see my way into his safety. It was then that I despaired, however brief, and I looked at my son, who stared back at me with the most trusting gaze, a look of pleading: *Mom, make me safe again. Mom, I'm scared,* and I thought, *Lord Jesus, I hate you more now than I ever have before,* and before I could even turn back to put the smaller trach tube in, Preston had taken the tube from me and he had gotten it into Jack's neck. "It's in, it's in," he said. We pulled the tie around his neck. Preston suctioned the trach until all the secretions were clear instead of pink, until the blood had subsided. We held him and kissed his head. Jack, so tired and brave, fell asleep immediately, his feet in their tiny giraffe faces dangling from either side of my right arm. We put him into his crib. Preston told the nurse that, as we had said before, no one should touch his trach but us. I went back into my room to try to finish pumping.

And then I understood what it is to despair. It is to look at your room lit by the warm reddish light, a pump pulling uselessly at your breasts, angry red marks still on them from where you pulled it off too early, and know that your son might have died in your house because the trach you gave him came out. It is to know that you, who used to take CPR in your high school in the same room where they held the school dances, needed in that moment to remember it. It is to know that your bones are shaking because your son, your firstborn, could be taken from you because of an airway that you went into the street, onto the water, up the mountain begging God to protect. Your son Jackson could die, and you knew this before; you knew this from the conference room broom closet; you knew this from watching the monitors in the NICU turn an angry red, the alarm sounding lower, two tones repeated endlessly until anyone, anyone came running. You knew this in the NICU, where danger was a well-accustomed guest.

And this is your home, and danger has invited itself in. And where was Michael, the archangel? Where is that legion of angels who had charge over Jack? Where is Jesus, who came so that all sheep can have life, and have it abundantly?

Jack didn't die, and some days I forget that Tuesday night, I forget the Indian food we abandoned, the friends we sent home, the way we held each other on the couch and cried and cried until we were as breathless as our son had been. Some days I imagine that there is a legion of angels keeping guard, keeping evil from our door.

But now I say *yet*. Now I say God has not let Jack die in my arms yet, because on a Tuesday night I saw my son turn pale and I saw him afraid and I saw how God might, how God could, take him.

When we lay in bed that night, Preston pulled me close. In his tears, he told me something I haven't forgotten. "Hilary," he whispered, his eyes bright like Jack's, but filled with a different fear. "I heard a voice say, 'The trach will go in.' I heard a voice behind me telling me to pick up the trach and put it in him." He shuddered and pulled me closer. "I think it was Jesus."

I want to say, *God has not let my son die yet,* but there was a voice behind my husband telling him to put in the trach. I don't know that Jesus will give me the luxury of saying *yet*. I don't know that I want him to.

★ ★ ★

Do you ever know when your beliefs die? Do they tell you ahead of time that they're going on life support? What are the signs of distress, the signs to call the doctor, the priest, the healer?

The first few weeks after Jack's diagnosis, I bit my tongue so much it bled, the iron taste almost sweet against my lips. I marched everywhere—upstairs, through our tiny apartment, around the block in my self-mandated pregnancy walk. I was furious but sure that if I kept praying long enough and hard enough, God would speak back. By that I always meant that God would undo it. I had ears for nothing but a do-over, a shift in the narrative.

I didn't know that the sweet metallic taste of iron, of the blood that kept not only me but also Jack alive, would be the taste of a dying belief. A belief that God would do whatever I asked, when I was asking for something good. A belief that I knew what God would do, deep down, when it counted. A belief, sweet and metallic all on its own, that perhaps all along I had believed in miracles but I just hadn't tried hard enough to practice my belief.

Here was the time to practice. But the belief in miracles, it was gasping for breath. It arrived, and it was gone at the same time.

★ ★ ★

At the second special ultrasound in June, our doctor told us that Jack's chin was not measuring as abnormally small as before. He actually forgot to mention it at all during the exam until Preston inquired. And then he seemed not to understand the question, to look at us strangely, before he remembered that list of names, *micrognathia*. He told us it didn't look too bad.

Preston insisted that we go out to lunch to celebrate. Here, *here* was the miracle, the start of the miracles. He posted on Facebook a thank-you note to our friends and family who had begun a big, bold work of prayer for Jackson, who even now were seeing the fruits of that prayer. "Keep praying," he told them. "It's working."

Preston went ahead of me much of the journey leading up to Jack's birth. He was on the water walking to Jesus. He bent the pages of prayer books; he preached that our son was already at twenty-two weeks the very image of God. He walked on, he kept walking, all those days and nights when I just sat on the bathroom floor or in his lap or lay awake in bed.

But my husband, he never just walked on ahead. He always turned around to see where I was. He called out for me, every day—*Hil, where are you?* Sometimes he sat down to wait for me and sometimes he came back, circled his arms around me. I've never been more seen than in those nine months, except all the months that have followed. I've never been looked for that way before, but that is how he looks for me every day.

Preston knew even as we pulled into the parking lot of Cracker Barrel that I wasn't there, that for me the miraculous was an empty category, an empty name. It was true that Jack's chin was measuring differently, and better, but I didn't believe it was a miracle. I believed it was a mistake corrected, a joke from God. What had we wanted all those weeks? To be told it was a misreading, a mistake. But it was all true, wasn't it? A mistaken measurement from one ultrasound to another (how big was Jack's chin even then? How was it possible to measure it at all?) was ironic, a sidelong look from God. But I refused to fall into believing again, and I refused to say that honestly.

So I cried; I said I believed. I ordered chicken salad. I drank raspberry lemonade. I smiled and tried to rejoice, the dust in my throat thickening the words as they came out. Preston knew. We stayed in the car outside Cracker Barrel for a long time before we went in. Once inside, he held my hand; he let me give myself away slowly, twirling my straw too long and letting all the ice melt in the glass, making a puddle on the table. He waited for me to admit that I did believe and I didn't. That belief was threaded with fear now, a fear of the cruel joke, a fear of the disappointment.

"I don't want to be disappointed in Jack," I said on our way home. "If we don't get the miracle, I mean."

"God doesn't work like that, Hilary," Preston said. "He isn't cruel."

I want to tell the story simply. I want to say that belief died when Jack was first diagnosed. Yet it resurrected every Sunday; it came back to life and kept bringing me back to life too. This happened every few days, and then every day, and then what felt like every hour. The belief ran so deep in me it was my blood, pumped in and out of my heart, a river of belief swelling under my skin.

I imagine now, looking back, a more elegant story for myself and my confrontation with God. I imagine myself in the corner of the boat where Jesus is sleeping. I imagine the sound the wind might make as it pushed up against the old, tired wood planks, how it would whisper its destruction and the waves would gather gleefully. I imagine how the boat would sink into the water and rise up again, teetering on the edge of the spray. I imagine myself screaming for Jesus. Jesus would wake up, rebuke the storm, go back to bed. The ordinary being of God and his creation. The everyday rebuking of all that seems sure to destroy, harnessing it back to fruitfulness.

It wasn't at all like that.

It was death and resurrection every day. I clung to Jesus. I jumped out of the boat. I bit my tongue. I got on my knees.

My belief in God has died and resurrected too much to measure. It endures because it dies and comes back to life. Believe what you know, some philosophers say, *believe what you know*. I know God, but belief is different than knowing. I'm still trying to imagine myself in the boat when Jesus calms the storm, calmed by his command. I'm still trying to get the taste of iron out of my mouth. I'm still trying to believe what I know—that God is, that God is good.

Chapter 7

PHILOSOPHY

In the summer, about two months before Jack's arrival, I waited outside my philosophy department's building for Preston to pick me up from a day's reading. The afternoon sweltered; my maternity clothes clung to my skin, a sweaty cocoon. I was studying medieval philosophers at the time—Aquinas, Scotus, Ockham—and as I waited, I suddenly knew what to pray. It was Aquinas and Scotus, those faithful friends on the road of God's love, who talked about God's infinity with a philosophy that bled into poetry and ended in prayer, who taught me to call Jesus "our way of going to God." The reading that day—from Aquinas, I think, but they have blended together—was about God doing all things immediately, though he chooses to do them mediately, through nature, through secondary causes.

God is the first cause, the reason the universe has existence. The things that work in us, around us—photosynthesis and reproduction, the change of seasons, the emotions of love—those are things that God chooses to do through other causes, but he can do all of them immediately, himself. He can be the cause of things that nature normally causes.

"Lord Jesus." I paced in a precise square, staring down at my belly. "Lord Jesus, you can do immediately what nature didn't do this time. You can create an eye. You can create an ear. You can close a cleft. You can bring into existence what did not exist and what nature didn't do this time. O Lord God, by your power I declare that you can do this for Jackson. You can do it immediately—no mediator. You can do it immediately—now. Please, God. Please show up and do this immediately."

It was the first time I understood what I was working to believe about God. I was trying to believe that God was capable. I was trying to believe that God really could do the things that he says he did. I have read the Bible often, but I haven't always read it for the purpose of believing the words themselves. I am good at the ideas of the faith; the words, the sentences, the stories they tell, this is harder for me. I can believe in the Resurrection, know it intimately, and yet not know what it means, concretely, for Jesus to have been raised with his scars. I can believe in healing, but I don't know what it means that Jesus spat in the mud and made someone see.

This was my prayer to begin believing that Jesus could do anything, or everything, or just this one thing.

★ ★ ★

My first three weeks in graduate school, I cried weekly. I had applied to the program on the hunch that I might enjoy philosophy, even though I had taken only the minimum number of courses in the material. I had taken plenty of ethics and one class in epistemology, but the words *metaphysics* and *philosophy of mind* still sat strangely on my tongue. I hadn't thought I would get in. I hadn't thought I would go. I was ready for history, for early modern Europe between the two world wars, for intellectuals like Jacques Maritain and their friends. I was going to build my life in the past, make a safe haven against the cold winds of ideas.

The momentum of God is faster than my own, and I was carried along it, to the graduate preview weekend on the wings of the last seat on the last plane to leave Boston before a huge snowstorm. I was carried along to the acceptance phone call during dinner with my parents and brothers laughing at me as I nervously paced up and down our living room. I was carried along to say yes, choosing classes while picking up bridesmaids for my wedding at the airport, classes with heavy names like Philosophical Writing and Recent Work in Virtue Ethics. I was carried up to the door of graduate school and then (it seemed) dropped.

Three weeks into the philosophical writing seminar, I was convinced that I would never understand analytic philosophy. My professor set us a variety of responses to the Sleeping Beauty problem—a problem about coin tosses, amnesia, and credence—and expected us to give précis of the arguments without faults. I swore heavily in our apartment on a Saturday afternoon about the problem, about how it didn't seem to matter whether she was one-third or one-half confident that the coin toss came up tails, given that she woke up and was told that it was Tuesday. It didn't seem to matter if, and how, it worked. I thought people believed or didn't, knew or didn't, and what mattered was what we did with what we knew.

I don't know what switched in the fourth week. Perhaps the momentum of God picked me up again. Perhaps it was that and finally getting an A on a reflection paper in ethics. Perhaps it was that I decided to stop being afraid that philosophy would show me up, best me—and I started to want it to. Slowly, I wanted to be bested by the best thoughts of other people. I wanted to come up against an idea and grapple with it, struggle to understand it, struggle to fit it into the world. And it was in this semester, in this writing seminar, with this professor (who remains one of the best professors I've ever had) that I first read Elizabeth Barnes.

It happened accidentally. Our second paper of the course was supposed to be one based on a piece of literature we were familiar with. I didn't have such a piece, so I chose to write on disability. I came to it not knowing the long literature in ethics or the material in sociology or anthropology or biology. I had this love of ASL and a longing to figure out if there was a way to connect them. And so I searched our library catalog and found "Valuing Disability, Causing Disability," an article that Elizabeth Barnes published in 2014.

I read it twice and took it home to Preston and told him that I had found a philosopher whom I wanted to imitate. I reread it, went back and read two other articles she'd published, and looked up most entries in her bibliographies. I pressed and pressed and pressed into a small but growing literature advocating a disability-positive view. It seemed immediately intuitive to me— our bodies do unexpected things; this is a way of being different in the world—and I finally wrote up a paper arguing that disabilities do not count as evidence of evil.

They are differences, as Elizabeth Barnes says, but they are merely differences. They don't carry any sense of being good or bad within them; they just *are* in the midst of someone's life, and the fullness of that life lends color and shape and meaning to the differences written in the body and the mind.

This is how God has worked, doing some things immediately and others in hidden and unexpected ways. Long before Jack was a whisper on the air or a positive test result, I found myself reading about disability, my mind reshaping itself. Reading Elizabeth Barnes widened my imagination about being a philosopher; infinitely more importantly, it made being Jack's mother possible. Elizabeth Barnes's articles, and later her book, a piece of the hem of Jesus's robe. A piece I didn't know I was holding on to until so much later, when I thought I had missed him altogether.

★ ★ ★

I presented my paper twice while we were early in pregnancy and Jack was smaller than a mustard seed. I was surprised to learn that there are sharp divides, that we often think we know the answer to questions of disability even when we haven't thought much about it before. Lots of people told me that they found my view to be obviously false, but intriguing. Others told me it was incredibly worthwhile to write and work on this question because it struck them as obviously true. I'm not sure whether there is anything obvious in philosophy. This view of disabilities, where they are differences, where they are not automatically bad, it was intuitive and it had the weight and feel of truth in my bones. That's what I knew—all I knew—until the phone call. Until the twenty-week ultrasound.

And it has this weight and feel in my bones still. It feels like an unorthodox approach to philosophy to go based on a feeling of truth in my bones. How do I know what the truth feels like? How do I know I'm in proximity to it, that truth is even the kind of thing you can be said to be closer to? But I don't know another way to do philosophy. My bones were what carried me through the six weeks of the NICU. My bones held me up as I sat in metaphysics class unsure whether it mattered anymore if time was real or not, since it had long abandoned me in those clockless rooms and hallways. My bones, fragile as they are, seem to be what I return to, sounding ideas out in between ribs, along my shoulder blades. And this idea—that disabilities are differences, complicated, hurtful beautiful good and difficult differences, like so many differences that make each of us alive as ourselves and not someone else—it still rings true.

I've read before that a disability is a gift from God because it teaches us something about weakness, or something about our own limitations, our own lack of ability before God. That kind of explanation still thinks disability is a bad thing, a thing that needs explanation, and it offers us this explanation about weakness and limitation.

I do not believe that disabilities need that kind of explanation. I do not believe that God creates children with physical or intellectual differences as object lessons for our spiritual maturing, that God's restoration of creation to himself means that, necessarily, everyone will have bodies with two ears and two eyes. I don't know what those who sleep in the dust will rise to be. I know Jesus is raised with his scars, his open wound where he will ask us to put our hands, to feel his flesh and know him anew. I know this is a sign of the new creation.

But fundamentally, I don't think God needs to give us a reason for disabilities. I want one, I have asked for one, but in the end I don't think there will be an accounting of why disabilities happened. I don't think they're part of the fall, though I do think some kinds of pain are. I don't think they're bad things in need of explanation. And this is the end of my philosophy—to find a way to talk about disabilities that tells a bigger, more surprising truth, a truth I am learning to believe. I'm looking for a way to describe and understand them, woven as they are into the fabric of bodies and minds, not as evil things that God permits because he has some good hidden reason, but as different things that God permits because God makes a wildly varied creation, because God knits us together, because God is present and intimate with us.

Maybe you ask here about all the disadvantages that accrue from having a disability. I ask that too. Our last morning in the NICU, an occupational therapist told her student that Jackson's condition made him "significantly disenfranchised," that he would have so much to overcome, but she said that he was nonetheless her favorite patient because, well, his cognitive development didn't seem impaired. I was putting Jack in his going-home outfit. He kept kicking his feet into my hands the way he has from the beginning. *I am furiously, joyfully alive in this body, Mom. I am not waiting for a more "normal" body to be this alive.*

The answer about the disadvantages is complicated. I know so little about different kinds of disabilities; there is so much to be written, so much to be learned. I do not know what it is like to live in a body that is different from mine—and it is so unlikely that different kinds of disabilities are similar enough to count them all the same. What Jack has isn't necessarily the same kind of thing that other kids have. Physical and intellectual disabilities are different from each other. Physical disabilities differ widely among themselves.

But I think about this often: A disadvantage connected to a condition is not always caused by that condition. Some disabilities are disadvantageous because of other things—the environment and community we're in, the language and assumptions surrounding that condition, the access—that aren't intrinsically part of that condition itself. We do not live in a world where every building is wheelchair accessible. Assuming that it is intrinsically harder to move through the world in a wheelchair is to mistake a surrounding limitation for an internal one. We do not live in a world where sign language is used proficiently by everyone; assuming it is intrinsically harder to be deaf is to mistake a limitation that comes from features of the world we are in for one that is part of the condition itself.

Not all the disadvantages will be explained this way. Not every story is one where the word *difference* is bigger than the word *hurt* or *suffering*. I worry as I write this that I'll spend too much time pretending that disabilities are simple, when they aren't. Rather, I want to make myself, to make us, pause. It is worth pausing when you meet people whose bodies are different, whose minds are different, to wonder whether you assume it is harder or more harmful because of that condition alone, when it very well might not be. I do not believe that Jack's differences are obstacles he will overcome. I don't believe that the mysteries of his missing eye and ear, his smaller chin, his cleft, are best thought about as *harms*. They are different; they are rare. But they also carry a certain kind of simplicity; they just *are*.

★ ★ ★

I stumbled over almost every sentence when I met Elizabeth Barnes at a philosophy conference the May after Jack was born. I was sitting next to her, and I hadn't been able to even eke out a hello until the end of the afternoon. I wanted to explain that her philosophy helped me mother my son. It taught me how to weave philosophy into something as delicate and complex as a new life. It taught me to be proud of him, to challenge my own worries and anxieties. Reading her philosophy—and the philosophy of the people she referenced, each slightly different in their challenges and insights—was catching sight of the hem of Jesus's robe even when I wasn't sure I could find it anymore.

She smiled at me kindly as I stumbled to explain this. She asked to see pictures of Jack. I showed her some of Jack smiling, that one eye blazing with mischief. In showing her those photos, I saw them as if for the first time.

This is Jack, I thought, *who brought all my philosophizing to its knees, who gave it purpose and life even before he was born.* There is good reason to think that heaven will have bodies wildly different from what we expect. Didn't Jesus rise with his scars, his open wounds? Isn't Jack's body something? Doesn't he look like Jesus?

Chapter 8

SPECIAL NEEDS

The day we found out that Jack had a cleft, I called my mother in the bathroom to say the words out loud, without any knowledge behind them. She didn't cry on the phone with me. She asked simple questions; she told me she loved me and Jack and Preston; she told me that we would keep doing the next obedient thing, because that is who we are. When I hung up with her, I stood in front of an icon of the Good Shepherd, sobbing. *What do I know about clefts, Jesus? What do I know about how this will change his life and change him? How will people look at him? What will they think? Isn't it wrong that these things are happening?*

Tell Jackson the story of his body. I bit my lip and tasted blood, the same blood, I thought at the time, that is keeping him alive. I'm sharing my blood with him, and it's my blood that's making him, building up bone and tissue and, now, a small gap running back through his mouth.

"Jacks, your doctor just called us. You have a cleft lip and a cleft palate. Our bodies do unexpected things sometimes. Your lip and your palate didn't close the way we expected." I paused, swaying back and forth. "But, Jacks, every body is a gift from God. Yours, right in the midst of exactly how it is and what it looks like, Jesus loves."

Maybe you wonder why I prayed for healing if I believe so firmly that Jack's life is not made worse by his having craniofacial microsomia. I wonder this too. Perhaps there is hypocrisy in it, and perhaps there is truth. Jesus told me to tell Jack the story of his body, and Jesus told me to get out on the water and pray. And every night after we prayed Compline and Preston fell asleep, I would whisper again, "Why did this happen to us?" And Jesus—it must have been him, mustn't it?—spoke back: *When you tell Jack the story of his body, of his life, don't leave anything out. Including me.*

★ ★ ★

We took pictures of Jack's first smile, the one that lit his face and split it open in joy, the smaller side of his cleft curving back in laughter, pulling his right nostril with it, for two hours the day before his lip surgery. "Remember this first smile," people told us. "You'll miss it more than you think." We saw glimpses of his smile two or three days after the surgery, his lip heavy under surgical glue, bruised and stitched, fighting to tell us of his delight in life, in us, in the yellow plastic lion with the bright red mane that twirls around and makes a clicking noise. His full, new smile arrived a week after surgery, on his changing table, his face lighting up in just the same way, his lip now stretching wide but holding together, new and not new at the same time.

Jack's life is not good *despite* his cleft. I want to make that clear, so clear you can see to the bottom of it. Jack's life did not start out good, get bad, and somehow come out good despite the bad. It is a rough-and-ready way to think of disabilities, to think they are *bad things* that must be overcome, that there is a calculus to quality of life, and the disability, the difference, is on the wrong side of it. It's a shorthand for our incomprehension, for that lack of imagination we run into over and over. I completed comps in the midst of a high-risk pregnancy; we survived forty-three days in the NICU; we made an ark of our arms around each other and Jack, things we never imagined until we lived them. Saying that Jack's life is good despite his cleft, his one eye, his one ear, his craniofacial microsomia, is too cheap.

Because that first smile was the most gorgeous thing I have ever seen in my life, gorgeous because, not despite. He smiled at me for the first time on his changing table while I was singing a song my mother used to sing to me, an old song from the days we lived in England on my dad's sabbatical one year. "Someone brought a jar of jam, someone brought a jar of jam, someone brought a jar of jam to put on the harvest table!" Jack paused, his eye wide and already laughing, and kicked his legs furiously up and down and up and down as I tried to fasten the two sides of the diaper on him, and then he smiled.

And I'm not a special needs parent who thought something otherwise terrible became beautiful in its own special way. I'm not seeing Jackson through magical glasses that blind me to how it really looks. Jack's smile is the most gorgeous thing, a smile lit with love and delight and the kind of joy that runs out to meet you, to welcome you, to teach you what you have long forgotten about the world. The way that smaller side of his lip wrinkled back, the way his nostril went up a little bit, as if he were inhaling the smells of the world, the way his eye scrunches up and how he smiles with his whole body, how if you kiss the small bit of origami skin on that right side, he squeaks and squirms and smiles even wider. That is what is most beautiful to me.

It is a pattern, and it is important. We take the cheap way of explanation, the simplest account. A disability is a lack, an absence, a "blight," one philosopher wrote, on an otherwise flourishing life. To make it right, God (or the body, or the social calculus, or something unnamed) must compensate. There must be some special lesson they teach us that we couldn't learn any other way. There must be some things they can do that they couldn't do without the disability, and those things justify the otherwise bad condition. We don't do well holding in our hands an uncategorized truth, and so we try to sort it. We are inclined to think that blindness is bad, but we then hear about the richness of someone's experience of blindness. How do these fit together?

Disabilities are hard to understand. They change and build and break down and utterly undo and complete lives. I don't know much about what Jack's life will be, and if I am honest, it is his to tell me what it is like, not mine to know. I can slip the trach tube in and out; I can swipe a sterile cotton tip applicator across the empty eye socket; I can kiss that small bit of extra skin. But I must wait for Jack to show me his life, to invite me inside it. And we must all wait, I think, to be invited in, and take off our shoes, for we stand in the presence of another human life and it is sacred, a creation, and a gift. And I can't believe God is a God who makes that gift good *despite* its differences. God makes it good *because* of them, *in the midst of* them. God makes that life good.

It is too easy to say that the cleft was bad, so his life without it is better. The cleft is too complicated for that. Jack's repaired lip is a new beginning for us. Once in the throes of our new life, Preston asked me how I could want the surgeries for Jack if I really believed in the mere-difference view of disability. Jack was asleep in the fuzzy lamb seat that friends of ours had lent us. We were sitting on the couch, watching the rise and fall, rise and fall of his chest. I stuttered. It was a good question.

"I think the cleft is a difference that has costs to it. I think the costs of having it are complicated, limit Jack in ways that don't seem right to limit him when the repair would do a lot of good. I don't think it is wrong to want the good that will come out of the surgery even though I don't think the cleft is bad in itself, the thing to be un-done. It is what it is; its costs are its costs, and we have to weigh, and we have to choose."

I am editing myself here. This is what I wanted to say. I think I cried and said something about how I think it's okay to want the surgery, but I wasn't sure how. I'm still not entirely sure how to want things like reconstructive surgeries when I believe so deeply that disabilities like Jack's aren't evil, bad things, but living, complicated things. But this is what I want you to see clear to the bottom of: that smile, that first smile, it was gorgeous because of the cleft. And Jack, in his blue denim shirt that his dad bought him for Christmas, bought so that they could match each other on Sunday mornings, and his little gray pants and his bare feet, his one blue eye catching all the light the day held, that day we took all those pictures: He was gorgeous. His smile—splitting his face with joy, shattering every thought of *It's so bad that this happened to him*—entered my heart and I have never been the same.

★ ★ ★

We were in our favorite café, Megg's, with Jack after a dentist appointment. An older woman drinking the dregs of her tea was sitting at the smaller table next to us, and Jack, curious as ever, stared at the world from his car seat propped in the chair next to his dad. His excitement generates secretions, and Preston turned on the suction machine we take with us everywhere.

"What is that?" Her question was unceremonious and, in most contexts, rude. Preston smiled, because he is the more gracious one of us. "This is a suction machine. Jack has a tracheostomy, so this lets us just suction out his secretions."

She looked perturbed. "Oh." I started to stare hard at

the Trivial Pursuit cards the restaurant leaves on the table to entertain the guests. All baby boomer cards, guaranteed to be a flop for the two of us, but I could feel her curiosity and pity traveling toward me, and all I wanted to do was throw it back at her. Preston sat down, still unbothered, and began to look at the menu.

"Well, it could be worse." I can't remember how she got to that line, whether she said much or little, but I remember that. We had ordered the deviled eggs and the empanadas, favorites from the days when Megg's was the only place we felt like eating while Jack was in the NICU. I had asked for a Coke, something I hardly ever do, and we had been talking a bit, Jack on his way to a nap.

We smiled half-heartedly. "Yes," we said. And it was true, but isn't it strange how people often tell you that it could be worse because they see what to them seems so bad that only a worse thing could be comforting?

"My grandson has Down syndrome." At this point I became angry at this stranger who wouldn't leave, who wouldn't take her bill and leave her empty teacup, and our family, in peace.

But Preston looked calmly back. "There is nothing wrong with having Down's." He said it simply so that it hung in the air, between them, the woman's mouth opening and closing a few times, catching her breath.

"You're right," she said. "He is so sweet."

We lapsed into a kind of uncertain silence. She nodded at her empty cup, as if to remind herself again that, yes, her grandson is beautiful and, yes, someone she doesn't know, who isn't in her family, had affirmed that too. Finally, she got up and wandered to the cash register with her bill gripped tightly in her hands, her credit card half-hidden under the blue rivers of her raised veins.

Preston smiled at me and looked at Jack. "Hilary," he said.

I forced a smile. "I'm fine. Let's order." He knew I wasn't, and I knew he knew, but he was kind enough to wait until the car ride home to bring it up.

"I just...Jack isn't broken." We'd shut the car door and were winding our way back toward the highway, toward home. "Why do people act like he is? Why can't they just say that he is beautiful?"

"People need help understanding."

"Well I think they should just try harder."

I'm not charitable enough when it comes to how my son teaches others to see the world. I expect that when someone meets him, they'll either ask us thoughtful, astute medical questions about his condition or coo at his smile, which takes up almost his whole face. I expect them to notice his blue eye, how it has a deep blue outer circle and a gray-blue inner one. I expect them to see the giraffe feet of his pajamas poking out from his car seat and squeeze his little toes.

I don't know whether these expectations are fair, or even right. I wonder often whether I am also playing pretend with myself, expecting that people won't notice his absent right eye, his small cheekbones, his slanting chin. These are as much part of Jack as the blue-gray eye, the endless smile. I think I might shy away from the reality that God made him beautiful within his body, not in spite of it. That God beholds, names, and claims for himself Jack's small, closed eye socket and those small cheekbones, the small tag of skin where an ear folded in on itself, a piece of origami, a body's creative answer to something unexpected. I have been hiding from how beautiful God thinks Jack is, wanting others to ignore what makes him different. I am so desperate for people to treat him "just like any other baby" that I forget he is Jackson David. He is the gift from the gracious God. He is God's beloved friend.

★ ★ ★

There is no community right to grieve over kids like Jack. We assume there is; we assume that we can sit in a coffee shop or after church or meet them on the street and assume that we can share a pitying glance, a compensating smile, a "well, there are worse things." I've been told that there are worse things than Jack's condition. I've been told that Jack's condition is the thing that is worse than something else. I've had people start out curious and quickly move to mournful. I don't think it's malicious.

But it is wrong. Our communities do not have a right to grieve that which is different simply because it is beyond the realm of what we have thus far imagined. Meeting Jack should be a call to widen your imagination about things like food and breath. It isn't something we mourn. That Jack had it a bit easier we do wish. When he pulls his trach out accidentally and is really scared and upset, can't catch his breath, when he sends me and Preston into a rush to do everything they taught us in the hospital, then we wish deeply that we had been given something else, something different, that Jack didn't need these things. That he didn't run the risk of pulling out his G-button and hurting himself or that he could be thrown into a pool in the middle of a Texas summer without thinking about it.

My wishing some things easier for Jack has never meant that I think the trach makes Jack worse off, makes Jack pitiable, makes Jack less. There is so much to him, and the tube is so small by comparison.

Here is why I think there is a difference between myself as Jack's parent and the wider community. As Jack's mom, I am wired to protect him. Anything that is harmful or has harmful repercussions for my son I want to defeat and do battle with. Even those things I *know* in my bones would be good for him, even physical things I know are merely differences. I know that it was good for me to have been picked on in school; I know it is something I wouldn't trade. But I don't want Jack to be picked on. I don't want Jack to have surgery even though I know surgery also helps him. I want Jack to have two eyes or two ears or no cleft or none of it. And then he kicks his feet up in the crib and I remember that wishing those things is not grieving their absence. And another person's noticing those things is not license for their judgment that his life is so much harder, that he has it so much worse.

And there is a difference, I think, for kids like Jack who are born without an eye and an ear, because for them it is not loss—they didn't lose it in an accident. They've come into the world this way, and their brains are therefore adapting from the first minutes to their environment to use the equipment they've been given, to live well as themselves, in their body. You should see the way my son smiles at the sight of his red fox, his dad's face, his hands. You should see how much of life he doesn't miss.

A few weeks ago I was on the phone with my former counselor, telling her the stories of the fall. Jack's birth, the diagnosis, how it was so much worse, so much more, than what we had imagined. "But you know what I hate the most? I hate that people pity him. That they feel bad for me. That they are sorry this is happening." My voice was flavored with resentment, that pent-up, bursting-to-escape confusion and anger. She didn't miss a beat. "But why do you think compassion is pity?"

I paused, unsure what to say. "Well, they keep saying they're sorry."

"But how else can they express compassion to you? Why do you think they're pitying you?" She paused, the further thought already well formed. I could hear it coming from the way her breathing changed on the phone. "I know you, Hilary. And Hilary doesn't like being pitied. But can you make room for compassion?"

I am stuck between compassion and grief, between wanting others to reserve judgment about Jack's life yet sit with me in what is hardest, what is least like their own lives. I want them to rejoice in the craze of their normal and yet not pity us for ours. I want people to feel grateful, but not guilty or grieving. I want too much from others.

I think this is also because I have always wanted too much from myself. I want to be Jack's defender, his advocate, his champion. I want him to hear every day of his life that he shows me Jesus risen in glory and not the Jesus who suffers, who rises with scars and open wounds.

I have never cried the way that I did the day that Jack's trach came out accidentally and we had to work fast to keep him breathing. I have never raged the way I did, my head on the overbaked dashboard of our car outside our hotel room, asking Jesus to please take this away, make it as if it has never been, come to our house, skip the widows and the aliens and the orphans on the way, forget the other people you have been planning to heal, and run to us, give me something miraculous, some story to tell.

Jesus is a man of sorrows who rises in glory to make those sorrows glorious. Jesus is acquainted with grief so that our grief may be acquainted with his life. I do not understand this. I write the words so that someday I might believe what I know to be true. Perhaps it is not good philosophy—that I might know and not believe—but perhaps it is truer than any philosophy I've read. Jesus, the man of sorrows, will wed this grief to his life.

★ ★ ★

A professor saw me outside a coffee shop partway through the summer of my pregnancy with Jack. I had sent the email to the department, explaining about the complications we had discovered, and hidden my computer away from me for the rest of the day. The professor was eating a breakfast taco. He hugged me and Jack, then pushed his baseball cap up and off his forehead, wiped away the sweat, put it back on. I sat down at his table. He took a few bites, telling me about his summer, and then he looked at me, teared up. He patted my hand. "What you're doing, it's remarkable." I was embarrassed, so I just stared at him awkwardly. "You're heroic."

The June sun was blazing and hot against my skin, my belly rippled with Jack's morning calisthenics. I could feel my shirt clinging to my body. I said something defiant about how hard it is to even imagine not having him, how heartbreaking, the strangeness of the language around abortion in these cases. My mind had run ten thousand miles from the coffee shop, a thousand miles from this man and his breakfast taco and baseball cap and kindness. I was thinking about the boy kicking in my body. I was thinking how unheroic it was, how I didn't want to be the hero because I had a baby other people wouldn't have or couldn't imagine having. I didn't want to be a hero, because Jack's being alive was not an extra burden that Preston and I were heroically bearing. His life was not our challenge, our sorrow.

After Jack had been home from the NICU for almost two months, we went to a wedding. At the rehearsal dinner, an older man smiled at me as Preston hoisted Jack, in his car seat, and walked through the room. Jack was wearing his nasoalveolar molding device (otherwise known as a NAM)—which helped bridge the gap in his lip before surgery. He learned quickly how to pull it out of his mouth and throw it at us. His eye socket was still goopy, the result of a staph infection that we were treating with erythromycin, which we still use to keep the bacteria at bay. I think Jack was smiling, because Jack always smiles at Preston. The older man leaned in. "I'm so glad that you didn't choose the way of death for him," he said to me as he patted my arm. I stared again. The suction bag was heavy in my hands; my heart plopped somewhere inside it.

I must deal with harsh realities. Cleft lip diagnoses are one of the top reasons for abortions in the United Kingdom. Babies born with trisomy 21—Down syndrome—are aborted at high rates in the United States and other parts of the world. If you google "disability and abortion," as I did, you'll find debates about just this question, of aborting babies because of a diagnosis in the womb. The older man, his hand on my arm, is likely all too aware that I might have chosen the way of death, as many do, and that it is a choice at all.

I served as a teaching assistant for a philosophy class the spring after Jack returned from the NICU. One week, we considered the rise of reproductive technologies, including those that allow for prenatal genetic diagnosis.

The students wondered whether this had the possibility of changing how we value the lives of those with disabilities, how we see them or talk about them. I looked hard into their faces and my voice was harsher than intended. "But I think it already has, don't you?"

Isn't this how we think of and talk about "special needs kiddos" who are so full of worth even despite these abnormal, imperfect lives they have? Isn't this the language we use, that parents are brave for choosing life for a child with a disability? And aren't we always thinking, *Other things being equal, it is worse to have a disability than to not have it*? That is on a website that is a guide to ethics from the BBC. It's in all kinds of literature on medical ethics, philosophy. I have read it often, even before Jackson was announced to us, and long before we knew he would have some complications. Aren't we always thinking it would be better for the child to not have the disability, better for the parents, better for the world?

And it is this I will spend my life challenging. This that I worry most is ahead for Jackson. Not that he will think we almost didn't have him but that he will be told that he should wish himself different, his life different, his life with an eye and an ear and perfect, normal hearing and vision. We wouldn't be the people we are without the bodies we have. But different is not worse. Abnormal, outside the norm, is not worse. And truth be told we'll often use quotations around those words—"abnormal" or "imperfect"—but I think we fear that it's really true, that our stories are stories of kids who didn't come to us as we wanted or expected. We fear their lives really are imperfect, less good, less normal, less...whatever they ought to be. And so we fill our spaces with words about them, about these special kids, about these precious angels God has sent us.

But we might also simply question that idea that their lives are worse. We might more simply hold to be true that lives are different, and our lives are different. I might have smiled at my professor and demurred from being called "heroic." I might have smiled at the older man at the rehearsal dinner and said, "I'm so glad Jackson is my son." I might just as easily have lived the philosophy I'm trying to argue. And I have already failed heavily at living this philosophy, which makes me think it must be worthwhile; it must be real.

Jack's needs aren't special; they're just his. He needs a trach. The trach, to function well, needs to be changed, the stoma wiped, the skin cleaned. He needs a G-tube. To call these "special" is to hide behind a word we think will make it sound like we especially cherish Jack, but really all it does is reinforce that his needs aren't like other kids' and that they're harder, more complicated, things we wouldn't wish to do for anyone. When we refer to children as "special needs," we have a difficult tendency to put them together, in classrooms, in playdates, in our minds. Jack has "special needs" or "is a special kiddo" and so are boys and girls with Down syndrome or Treacher Collins syndrome, children who are congenitally deaf or blind or who use a wheelchair. Jack's medical condition isn't very similar to any of the aforementioned. Craniofacial microsomia is rare; his internal organ structures and function look similar to someone without craniofacial microsomia. He has some complications with hearing and sight, but they don't resemble being deaf or blind. He may develop skills on a different timeline, but he is different from children with cognitive disabilities.

And this is going to hold true, in general, for kids who for some reason or other have what has traditionally been considered special needs. Not much of what different people have by way of difficulties or challenges or alternate ways of doing something (eating, speaking, etc.) will really resemble each other enough for us to make one category and one classification out of them.

These radical, transformed lives. These wild, beautiful, difficult lives. I am so glad I did not choose the way of death for Jack. I am distraught that I could have. His life, nothing like what I had thought. Nothing like a cleft lip. Nothing, and everything, special.

Chapter 9

CONFRONTING GOD

It was never hard to believe that Jack brought with him the Kingdom of God. People told us all the time that he was a treasure, that he had a special mission from God. Some people believed it was the compensation for his disability; some believed it was the reason for his disability. Some, I hope, believed it had nothing to do with his disability. But it was not hard to believe Jack was a treasure. I glowed throughout my pregnancy with Jack, and he delighted at kicking the hands of well-wishers when they asked to feel him move. I believed all along that Jesus was terribly, irrevocably thrilled at creating Jackson.

It was me I couldn't believe it about. Me, the vessel, the cocreator and helper of the Almighty bringing my son forth from nothing. It was me I couldn't believe God saw as treasure; I was not the one sheep Jesus would leave ninety-nine others to find. It was my body this had happened in, and that meant that ultimately this hard new road was my fault. My uterus, my problem. My body, my error, however mysterious and impenetrable. I imagined that everyone blamed me, which no one did. I imagined most of all that God blamed me. It was easier to control the rage and sadness that way. If I was to blame, then God could remain preserved; God could still be good; God could still be the hero of the story. If I was the one who went wrong, God was justified in leaving us to our failing devices, our less-than-perfect solutions. If I had done something wrong, then God was not to blame for leaving me to solve it, riddle my way free.

It is a poor way to preserve God, and it failed for the last time at four in the morning when our nurse knocked on our door, our hearts waking up before our eyes, to tell us that Jack couldn't keep his oxygen saturation up above 80 percent without the oxygen tank we had, which was empty, without the spare tank, which was also empty. It failed for the last time when I sat in the back of the car flying down the deserted Waco streets, Jack half-awake, coughing constantly, and felt his cheeks and worried their coolness, their pale glimmer in the passing streetlights. It failed, finally, irrevocably, when the transport team brought back a child-sized stretcher and he shrank on it, his tiny self too tired to cry anymore, and we drove to the pediatric ICU in Temple.

Then I realized that I had not saved God from the depth of my condemnation. Then I realized that I had not emerged unscathed, my faith intact, my heart still pure. Then I realized it had ended, whatever had been before with me and God, whatever assumptions, presumptions, whatever knowledge. Then, as we unfolded clothes, as we drove to Target for jeans, as I plugged the hospital breast pump into the PICU wall and Preston gathered labels and bottles for measuring feeds, it failed.

It wasn't my fault all this had happened to us, this danger, this flying down highways for oxygen. This wasn't mine, not the longing I had for my son, for his wild life. I wanted to be the pretty woman, with her pretty thoughts about God. I wanted to be the sweet and kind person, who held out the mystery and declared, *Be it unto me, Lord, according to thy word.* I wanted to keep resuscitating the relationship I had once had, to press the empty heart just one more time, just thirty more times.

But my heart lives flung up against the wailing wall, shouting at God that he owes me an explanation for this, that he owes me understanding. I am only this woman, who prays short and sharp and who begs one minute and rages the next. I am only this woman, who is right in the thick of the price of this great pearl of the Kingdom. "In his joy he went and sold all that he had and bought it." This is a hard teaching, for you must leave behind, sell, give away, even the beautiful old ways of being with God. You must empty your life of the empty metaphors you once loved and lived by. The PICU in January froze them. The silent highways burned them. The tired, fearful look in my son's eyes broke all their bones.

What can I say to God, what will suffice, what has it become between us?

★ ★ ★

This is how I ask the question of suffering now. I used to ask about theories, about how God's goodness could square with God's love, how different properties of God made sense in light of suffering. I used to read books about suffering and cry and wonder, in a safely academic way, how these stories make sense if God really loves us and really has the power to change the stories at any moment, to intervene in nature, to alter what looks to us inevitable.

It might seem like there is not a lot of explanation to be found. After all, hasn't God said in Scripture that his ways are not ours, his thoughts not ours, that so much higher are his ways and thoughts? Who are we—worms, dust, ashes—to ask God for an explanation?

Perhaps it seems that God's providence and provision are enough, that the words *God is King* conclude with a full stop. I'm glad if it is, for I think in the end, *God is King* will be the refrain. For at the name of Jesus every knee will bow.

And while I did get out on the water to pray for healing, and it didn't come, and I did pray for an easier way of breathing, and Jack's tracheostomy has meant both safety and danger—this question of suffering sits between me and God. I am still looking for a way to think and believe and talk about Jesus and the long-deserted streets of Waco with an empty oxygen tank. I think others might be too. I'd like to ask us together in the ragged band of lovers to imagine why. To sit ourselves down in the stories. Stories of suffering, heart's desire unfurled before God, desires for beautiful, good things—desires for children, for marriage, for meaningful work, for the chance to write a book, for a trip to Paris, for good health and safety, for some project we love to work at and succeed. These desires, I can't call them bad or sinful. I think they are desires after the heart of the Kingdom. To me, they are pearls of great value, things worth having and doing.

And sometimes they fail. The children do not come; the beloved dies; there is no marriage or a marriage falls apart. Jobs are lost or never found, books are rejected, there is no money for Paris, and there is sickness and danger. These dreams and longings, they collapse.

But God loves us. And God loves these good things we wanted and prayed about. God desires that our heart's desires be met.

And I don't think that means God aims to strip away from us anything but him, because Jesus is in the good things we were asking for. The joy and love of Jesus exist in the things we longed for.

But God is all-powerful and all-knowing, capable of anything, immediate or mediate. God can conquer cancer and joblessness and infertility. God can undo and rewrite and pull through and out of nowhere make all things be that can be so made.

But God is all-good, loving toward his children, desiring that none suffer, desiring that all be saved and not only saved but set free rejoicing and alive, most fully. "I am come that they may have life and have it abundantly," Jesus says in the Gospel of John.

These things—God's omnipotence, omniscience, omnibenevolence, perfect love—these things are what make suffering obscure to us. This is the veil cast between us and the agony of our lives, the veil we claw at so desperately when we suffer. "What profit is there in my death, if I go down to the Pit? Will the dust praise you? Will it tell of your faithfulness?" the psalmist asks. Impertinent and courageous. For our suffering is something we ought to ask an explanation for. Our suffering is something that demands satisfaction.

The book of Job ends with God speaking to Job. And it can seem as though God's answer is the real take-away from the story. But I think the story is there in part to show us that it is not just about what God says back to Job, it is also about what Job says to God. Job asks something of God. God grants Job the demand for satisfaction. God comes and speaks back to him. The point of Jacob's wrestle isn't merely the hip out of joint. It's also the hours, the not letting go, and the blessing. In French, the word *blessure* means *wound*. We will be wounded by the answer to our suffering, I am sure, but in the wounding is the blessing, and in the asking is the hope.

★ ★ ★

We lost our nurse early in December after Jack was born. I had been awake at 3:00 a.m. one night around Thanksgiving to pump milk for Jack, sitting alone with too many (or too few?) thoughts, when I heard the familiar beep of Jack's feeding pump. It's the beep that says "dose done" and it's a constant high-pitched beep, steady the way that yoga instructors always ask your breathing to be. A minute or two went by, and I thought the nurse was probably changing him, but of course that couldn't be the case because if he was feeding, he would have been in his crib. I didn't know what to think, but when I was finished pumping, there was the steady beep. I paced into the living room. I wanted to rush in and demand an explanation and at the same time I didn't want to disturb someone who might be doing her job. I'm his mom, yes, but his nurse seems like a title to tiptoe around, someone to be respected.

And then Jack coughed.

A cough isn't dangerous—Jack does it all the time in his sleep—but when there is something to be suctioned, it needs to be suctioned. He coughs to tell you that he needs you. And when I heard him cough, I heard him ask me to come be his mom, all my worries and insecurities be damned.

The nurse was asleep on the floor, her head on some of the quilts dear friends and family had made for Jack in the months before he was born. She was asleep, under Jack's blankets, and I had to shake her awake. I didn't look at her as she fumbled up and tried to act as if she were just dozing. I stroked Jack's hair and then told her I was going to go back to bed for an hour or two. I told Preston, and he got up and sat up in the dining room, ears and eyes trained on the nursery, keeping watch so that I could sleep.

We forgave the nurse that time. She apologized, explained it was a night she should have asked to not come, promised she understood the severity of it. But when I walked in again a few weeks later to the same situation, we fired her. The agency understood but couldn't find us anyone else to cover. So there we were, the days of December, sleeping in shifts in our bed. I would wake up at 3:00 a.m., watch the hours flicker until the sun came up, until Jack woke, my heart in a pendulum of confusion and joy.

It was in those late nights that I started to read the blogs. Baby after baby, clickable links for prayer buttons and names like "Miraculous Maggie" and stories of the wonder of medicine. Heart donors and successful transplants. Surgeries for scoliosis, clefts, kidneys. Medications that teach our bodies to accept the new organs or stitches. In those late nights I read blogs. I read blogs about kids with cystic fibrosis and hypoplastic left heart syndrome. I read about kids who needed transplants and kids who were on ventilators. The algorithms hummed even in the middle of the night; they knew that I was searching for stories like ours, stories that were not like ours, stories of hospitals and home health and conditions diagnosed when the baby was still just the size of a sweet pea or a yam.

I wanted to love these kids. I wanted to let these stories keep me open, undo the self-made stitches of nonchalant medical lingo I'd built up in the NICU. I wanted to be softened, made kinder by remembering that there are others who share this strange, and strangely beautiful, work. That is what I told myself while I clicked on post after post, the About section, the pictures. I want to read this because it will show me more about the wonder of the face of Jesus.

But how can I write this down? I read them for the relief of experiences more dire than my own. I read them for the reassurance that as desperate as I was at 4:00 a.m. listening to Taylor Swift and crying, there was some other mom somewhere who was having a hard time of it, a harder time of it. I told myself this would soften me, open me. And it did. And it also bound me, sharp suture needles night after night, scar tissue growing over the very places I believe I was meant to leave untouched.

I read blogs of people who were praying like we had for a miracle and waiting for baby boys to be born displaying the power and the handiwork of God. But how can I tell you this? I read their blogs and I was relieved when they didn't get their miracle, when God didn't take away their son's condition, because maybe it meant that after all God didn't do those miracles anymore. Maybe all of us are the house next door to Jairus. Maybe

Jesus doesn't bring healing with him for the house next door.

This is the truth, and it is not pretty, this sorrow and hope that circles us. Maybe you are reading this with the same thought—*that she, too, didn't get the miraculous healing Jesus did not bring me*—and if you are, it's okay. There is no condemnation for it, for this is walking to the wailing wall, this is getting into the dust of it, the cracked earth beneath our feet. I read, and I cried: for the kids, for the parents, for the fact that we don't understand the human body and that genes can arrange and rearrange and hurt us. And those long December nights I nurtured in me a secret relief, that I wasn't alone in the world of unanswered prayers. That I hadn't missed the quota of people who needed to pray a miracle into being. These live near each other, uncomfortable neighbors. I write that in the present tense, because it is still true.

I read and I pray. I pray for a healing I know Jesus can do, even now that he has chosen not to do it for Jack. I pray for courage that I forget I still need, for strength I've long since stopped demanding. I remind God that he can do all things immediately, even now. I pray, I lift up my voice even as I whisper in my sinking heart that I don't know what I will do if God answers my prayers for a baby other than my own.

★ ★ ★

"You have to give me a new way to find you, because the old ways have died," I shouted at God as I put on my blinker to turn right onto our street late one night, just about one year after Jack was born. "You let the old ways die and I have no way now. You have to give me a new way."

I pulled the car into our driveway, put it in park. I cried again, free to mourn the death of those old ways, their loveliness, their ease.

It wasn't your fault, Hilary.

He spoke it and I cut the engine, the music suddenly arrested into silence. "But will you give me a new way? Will I find you again?"

I swallowed, opened my car door, swung my legs and my body out. The air was warm. I shut the door, and in a silence I cannot describe, I walked along our front hedge, up the concrete steps, and stood at our front door, fumbling for my keys.

The door was already unlocked.

All that was left was to open the door, press my weight to it, and feel it give way.

This is what lies ahead. When I pray now, I remember the unlocked door, and I glimpse, so briefly, the shift of the hem of his robe as Jesus, side by side with me, presses on.

Chapter 10

PRAYER

We prayed Compline many nights of the second and third trimesters. We prayed it half-heartedly and devotedly, in bed and on the couch, our hearts overflowing and dry as the ground in February in my north-of-Boston hometown. Many of the nights Preston would pray it over me, my eyes drifting closed long before the psalms, the calls and responses, had finished. I wanted to pray these old words, but they felt like sawdust in my mouth. Preston used an old monastic diurnal, yellow and purple and green ribbons frayed at the edges to mark the confession, a collection for the feast day. My mother told me often that my pregnancy was prayer, that living with another human being inside my body was the same as entering the throne room.

In Compline we prayed Psalm 91, written in the following way:

Whoso dwelleth under the defense of the most high shall abide under the shadow of the Almighty.

I will say unto the Lord, Thou art my hope, and my strong hold, my God, in him will I trust.

For he shall deliver thee from the snare of the hunter, and from the noisome pestilence.

He shall defend thee under his wings, and thou shalt be safe under his feathers; his faithfulness and truth shall be thy shield and buckler.

Thou shalt not be afraid for any terror by night, nor for the arrow that flieth by day;

For the pestilence that walketh in darkness, nor for the sickness that destroyeth in the noon day.

A thousand shall fall beside thee, and ten thousand at thy right hand, but it shall not come nigh thee.

Yea with thine eye shalt thou behold, and see the reward of the ungodly.

For thou, Lord, art my hope; thou hast set thine house of defense very high.

There shall no evil happen unto thee, neither shall any plague come nigh thy dwelling.

For he shall give his angels charge over thee, Jackson,

To keep thee in all thy ways.

*They shall bear thee up in their hands, that thou hurt not
thy foot against a stone.*

*Thou shalt go upon the lion and adder; the young lion and
the dragon shalt thou tread under thy feet.*

*Because he hath set his love upon me, therefore will I de-
liver him, I will set him up, because he hath known my
Name.*

*He shall call upon me and I will hear him; yea, I am
with him in trouble, I will deliver him, and bring him
to honor.*

*With long life shall I satisfy him, and shew him my sal-
vation.* (Psalm 91, Monastic Diurnal)

Preston would add that single word—Jackson—every
time he prayed this psalm. *For he shall give his angels charge
over thee, Jackson,* as he laid a hand over the place where
Jack would kick or rub his elbow up against the limits
of my skin. There is something in the word *shall* that is
more forceful, more sure, than a mere *will. Shall* sounds
triumphant, declarative, a word for what the King does
and decrees. *Will* sounds small by comparison. He shall
give his angels charge over thee, Jackson. He will give his
angels charge over thee, Jackson. I used these old words
as a veil to my greater worry, the worry that grew in
me just as fast as the hope. Because each time we prayed
this psalm, I believed a bit more that Jackson would be

physically healed. Every time I reached the words *He shall give his angels charge over thee, Jackson*, I would feel the beat of their wings or the rush of the wind in which they travel (not unlike Mrs. Whatsit and Mrs. Who and Mrs. Which in *A Wrinkle in Time*). My heart kept quickening at the thought, those angels having charge over my son, there being many hands to bear him up, that no harm could come nigh him for this the King had declared he *shall* do.

Why was this so worrisome, but for how it drew me away from what is safe and comfortable? It was dangerous to pray so boldly because the psalmist doesn't spell out exactly what it is that God is going to do in giving angels charge over thee, Jackson. It doesn't say you won't have a cleft or an absence of an eye. It doesn't say that you will be born breathing like a marathon runner, lungs drinking in our air and screaming back life. It doesn't say that, so what does it say?

That "angels have charge over thee. That they keep thee in thy ways. That you shall not hurt your foot against a stone." The most common place the nurses looked for veins for the IV was in Jack's feet. He's been pricked and poked more times than I can hold in my mind, each time the small red drop a mere memory for him, but what is it for me? I kept returning to the psalm, searching for specificity, for a promise that held more in it. Night after night, as I would wake up sweating or freezing, my clothes strewn around me from never knowing what internal temperature I would be, I would stumble to the bathroom, my mind turning on Compline.

Compline does not end with the psalm, you see. There is more:

> *Thou, O Lord, art in the midst of us, and we are called by thy name. Leave us not, O Lord our God. Thanks be to God.*
> *Keep us, Lord, as the apple of an eye.*
> *Hide us under the shadow of thy wings.*

This I would say to myself as I stared into the bathroom mirror, listening to my husband sniffle in his sleep, the creak of the bed as he shifted, searching for me. *Keep us, Lord, as the apple of an eye. Hide us under the shadow of thy wings.* Only then, saying it out loud, could I fall asleep.

When we went to visit my in-laws the weekend of my birthday, the weekend after we learned about Jack's ear, Preston didn't offer to pray. I don't know if it was the combination of exhaustion, the weariness we wore and never talked about, not even to this day. It was work to bear with one another something so new and different, work to allow ourselves to hold in our hands the reality that this was happening to our beloved. I raged at the fact that my husband's first child had complications. I raged that his son had no eye, and no ear; I prayed earnestly to God to spare Preston in the same breath I prayed for God to spare Jack. Isn't it strange these prayers, the shape they take, the way they are answered?

We had been married only a year, you see. And that was a grief some people wanted to wear for us, a grief of a too-early introduction of sorrow, hardship, the navigation of thunderous waters in a raft we had only just begun building. Someone said to me that they were sorry for us, that we had so much to bear so soon. I was angry at this and overwhelmed at the truth of what they said. They shouldn't feel sorry for me, I raged, but they weren't wrong. Young marriage is young, that's the beauty of it. Preston and I fought long hours in car rides to and from his parents' house, learning the rhythm and weight of our pauses, how our voices rise and fall and just what we think it means when they do. We danced in the kitchen and we curled up on the couch and we cried long, desperate tears both apart and together. Preston bought us tickets home to Boston for Easter as a surprise just before we learned Jack's diagnosis. He is always doing things like that, to this day, wrapping me up in his arms or letting me sit on his lap in the dining room while our son, the one that people thought must be so hard on our marriage, sleeps.

But what I mean about young marriage is that Preston and I were learning how to wear our grief and each other's. My grief is often a thick woolen coat, insulation against the cold of not feeling anything, but heavy, deafening to other noises and other thoughts. I have to heave it on and off, and in the months before Jack was born I wore it around me, and asked Preston—more often without words, if I am honest—to be the one who helped me take it off, who helped me see the beauty of summer mornings and drives to Sonic.

Preston carries his grief like a well-worn pair of Toms, the kind that he wears into the ground with his pacing through the world. He builds on his grief, moves upward. It anchors him in some few moments but more often it goes along quietly, steady and present, unspoken. His grief is often unobtrusive, and often I miss it while I am struggling in and out of that thick woolen coat.

I didn't know this when we began and our love was fierce and new, and the light of Jack burned in that newness, hollowed out spaces for us to grow. I was so angry that my husband, and our new beginning, had to sit in a temporarily refurbished broom closet while the NICU doctor explained to us how the NICU worked, where Jackson would need to go when he was born and how they would monitor him, how they long to send babies home as soon as they can. I was so angry that she smiled at him across her Styrofoam coffee cup, that she existed, that there was a broom closet for parents of kids who will be born with complications. And my anger and my grief and my new marriage, they hung in the air that night in July, when Preston didn't offer to pray.

The lights were still on; we were each on our phones, a blanket of silence settling on us. You should know that I wasn't praying much at the time with Preston or on my own. I was putting on his shoulders the work of keeping us a praying people, a praying family. I had an endless conversation with Jesus, but it was solitary, silent, something I kept to myself in a corner of my heart hidden even from my husband.

So when I reached for the prayer book and began the familiar words, he was startled, his eyes glinting with tears. I led us through each prayer, saying the *Let us bless the Lord* so that he responded, *Thanks be to God.* We held each other a long time before we fell asleep. He put his hand on my belly, and I said it again, for all of us: *He shall give his angels charge over thee, Jackson, to keep thee in all thy ways.*

Day by day, we prayed Compline. Day by day, we burned away the shiny newness of our love and planted seeds in the dark corners. Day by day, we showed each other the shape of our grief and our joy, those thick woolen coats and old Toms shoes, and we tried them on, however faltering, however brief. To this day we each have our job when we change Jack's trach tube. I offered, the first time, to be the one who slipped it out and a new one in. I told Preston I didn't want to compare myself with him. That was true.

It was also true that I wanted to spare him that small work, the work of pulling out an airway and pushing in a new one. God spared him that. God spared me many things I know my husband begged him to spare me. And God sent doctors with Styrofoam cups of coffee, Compline, and Jack, to burn away and to begin.

★ ★ ★

There was one person I think prayed for me during my pregnancy more than any other. It's not Preston, though I know he prayed in unimaginable ways. I could see him, hear him breathing in bed when he thought I had fallen asleep, breathing his prayers, words left behind long ago, left behind at twenty weeks. No, the person I am thinking of is named David Lumsdaine. He was a professor at Gordon, the college where I did my undergraduate degree, a colleague of my dad's in the political science department and a fire of righteousness. That seems like the right thing to call him, a fire of righteousness, and a fire of kindness, a fire of faith. He glowed with a belief that made your belief deeper, more real to you. He loved Jesus in a way I had never encountered before in my life. He died suddenly of a heart attack a couple of years ago.

I didn't really know David Lumsdaine while he was alive. He had come to my house for backyard barbecues with the department; he had sat in my row at lectures; he sat in the pew two sections over and ten rows up at church. I knew who he was. I admired him, but I didn't befriend him.

When he died, they held a brief memorial service the next day in the Gordon chapel. I went and sat with my dad. I went to a small vigil that night at our church. The week of his death came and went. I remembered him fondly, when I thought of it, but I didn't think of him often.

And then Jackson was diagnosed with a cleft lip and palate, in that phone call on a Tuesday afternoon in April. When I had finished crying in the car, when I had called Deacon Lisa and implored the people of HopePointe Church to pray, when we finally came home, I stood in front of our icon of the Good Shepherd. I cradled my son in my belly and my belly in my hands, and I wept deeply, whispering again and again, *You are the lamb on his shoulders, Jack. You are the lamb. This is a picture of you and Jesus. This is a picture of you.* I told Preston that night in bed that I believed Jesus would and could do the miraculous. I believed that he would, and then I believed that he could. I said it in that order.

I returned to that icon so often that summer that I started to feel as if it were haunting me. It hung next to Martha, her arms stretched in hope and prayer. As is the case with most icons, Jesus's eyes followed me through the apartment, watching me as I moved through my day. When Jack was in the NICU, we brought both icons to sit propped in his crib, those eyes, those arms. Watching and hoping. The icon hangs in our living room now, still next to Martha. Jesus is still looking at me.

But there is something about this icon, you see. David Lumsdaine had the same one, only bigger, in his office at Gordon. When he died, the department chair, Ruth, organized his office belongings, and his closest friends—my dad among them—went through and chose items to bring home, to remember him by. My dad brought home that icon of the Good Shepherd. It took up residence in the "stove room," the room where my family gathers most, if not all, of the time in fall and winter, our twenty-year-old mugs holding tea and the big black Labrador always scrounging for food from someone. The icon does not demand attention there, but it keeps watch. When I lived at home before I married Preston, I would see it out of the corner of my eye sometimes, keeping watch.

So that Tuesday afternoon, weeping in front of the

icon, my hands on my belly trying to soothe a baby who was not in distress—I told myself this often, that Jack was never in pain, never frustrated, never afraid—I remembered David Lumsdaine. I saw him, more clearly than I could account for, saw his wild scraggly gray hair, his glasses slipping off the end of his nose, his pants always a bit loose at his waist and his untied shoelaces, his blue eyes, a gentler blue, his smile. I saw him, saw his face of concern, his understanding.

"Will you pray for me?"

I don't know if I can say I saw him do anything, because it wasn't a vision in the first place—it was a remembering, a knowing, a knowing that David Lumsdaine was near to Jesus, nearer than I could bring myself to be. So I asked, asked the dusty bricks where the icons hung.

"Will you pray for my son?" The last word a sob, a whisper.

I believe that the saints are attentive to us, that the veil is thin enough to shout through, that the cloud of witnesses is not above or below but near, a cloud that abides. I believe that David Lumsdaine prayed for me and for Jack more than anyone else. I believe he went before God on my behalf, that this man who is a fire of righteousness, who taught his students to befriend Jesus, who sat two sections over and ten rows up, listened to me crying before the icon that mirrored an icon he once owned, whose subject he saw face-to-face. I believe his prayers kept me breathing those last weeks of waiting. I believe he prayed that I would be a fire, too, a fire of believing and strength and hope. I believe he prayed me safely into the labor and delivery room. I believe in prayer because I believe he prayed.

One final story? We were driving back from Houston on a Sunday afternoon, and we took the long way home, going all the way up Route 6. Around the time that it turns to wide, flat grassland, where you see miles of sky spilling over the earth and nothing else is in sight, we were playing music, hymns, and I was remembering the words from growing up with a loyal-to-the-end 1982 hymnal: "In the sweet, by and by, we will meet on that beautiful shore." I didn't know the words except those, but I sang as I closed my eyes and the sun streamed in the windshield and I realized again that a man I had not be-friended in this life was somehow still caught up in the work of this pregnancy, this child's life, this hope or won-der or terror of waiting. *In the sweet by and by, we will meet on that beautiful shore.*

I cried freely, because I realized then, and I realize again now: I will meet David Lumsdaine on that beautiful shore. I will meet him and we will walk together, and I will tell him thank you. Thank you for praying for my son.

I can hear his voice, alight with kindness: "I was glad to, Hilary. I was glad to."

★ ★ ★

In the years before I married Preston, right after I graduated from college, I assisted in the children's Sunday school program at my church, Christ the Redeemer. The curriculum is called the Catechesis of the Good Shepherd, based on the work of Maria Montessori, based, perhaps most deeply, on the surprisingly wide and spacious hearts of children. In the Atrium—the name we use for the physical space where Catechesis happens—children encounter Jesus. And then they often turn back to you, hands wide, smiles wider, and give him to you.

In the Atrium, the room was set up with varying tasks—"works"—for the children to take on while they were there. A work is a space on a shelf with a task. Sometimes it's small clay figures and acting out a scene from a biblical story; sometimes it's two jars of water that you pour slowly, one into the other and back. Sometimes it is a tiny altar, just large enough for the uncertain hands to lay a fair linen, a paten, a chalice down and to have the catechist light the altar candles. We almost always asked the children, "Is there anything you would like to say to Jesus about this work?" and quite often they sang back praises for things in their worlds: dogs, sleepovers, horses, a birthday, the sun, the beach. Those Sundays of sitting cross-legged on the floor, watching as they pieced together the meaning of Jesus, of his life, of his ministry, taught me more about God than any Sunday I spent in grown-up church.

There are several small works for the three-to-six-year-olds to help them think about the parables of the Kingdom, and one Sunday morning I led a child through the work on the mustard seed. On a small wooden tray, there was a jar of mustard seeds and a magnifying glass and a small framed photo of a mustard tree under a hot Israeli sun. I don't know where we got the photo, probably from someone who has been there, touched and seen this vision of the Kingdom.

The lesson was simple, just a few laminated pages. Jesus said the Kingdom of heaven is like a mustard seed. Though it is the smallest of seeds, it grows into the greatest of trees and the birds of the air come and make a home in its branches. The little boy I was working with really only wanted to use the magnifying glass to look at everything but the mustard seed: his hands, the buttons on his collared shirt, the specks of dirt and grit in the carpet. I poured a few seeds into his palms, and as he held still, staring and squinting exaggeratedly to show me how very small they were, I read him the parable. Jesus said the Kingdom of heaven is like one of these seeds; though it is small at first, it grows into this great tree. The work tasked me, the assistant, with asking him the question: Is he small? How does he grow? Will he someday be bigger? Does Jesus help us grow? What would he like to say to Jesus about this?

The boy laughed and dropped the seeds onto the carpet. I hid my smile and went with him to the colored pencils and paper, where he drew a fire truck jumping off a mountain. I have never forgotten this question: *What would you like to say to Jesus about this?*

I would like to say that you let my son's body be broken before he had the chance to know it would bring you glory. I would like to say that your parables aren't for the wise-hearted; they're for the wistful who want to believe that something so small will always and inevitably become something so beautiful. I would like to say that you took from me the chance to ever walk away from you; showing up like you did all those weeks of waiting for Jackson, you took away the chance that I could become an unbeliever because I heard you—*I heard you say that you were the King*. I heard you say that you loved my son and knew him already. You took from me the dignity of unbelief, the simplicity of it, the story that ends with, "and I left the church because of suffering." I would like to say that you told a lot of stories about seeds to your disciples, but what about those of us who have lived so long on the vine we need something else from you, something different? I would like to say you gave me parables when I needed promises and you gave me promises, but I needed protection.

On Sundays in the Atrium, we always ended our time by being all together at the prayer table. We would light a candle, and one of the children would parade around the room with the rainstick to get our attention and call us together. We would sing familiar songs—"This Little Light of Mine" and "Like a Shepherd He Leads Us" and "I Want to Walk as a Child of the Light." And we would ask the children to name things they were grateful for, to pray thanksgivings, to tell Jesus things. The children were not afraid of the ordinary or the apparently irrelevant. They told Jesus about parties and pigs and the cold weather. They told him about how they liked to go on walks with their families by the river, how they were so excited to have a baby brother or sister. They said *thank you*; they said *I love you*.

I would like to say to Jesus: These days are warm and full of sunlight, and Jack has learned to roll from side to side. He makes noises like a dolphin over his trach, a language of his own, one I imitate to make him smile. He is always grabbing his red fox and the purple plastic beads from a Mardi Gras we never went to. He loves the bath, the brown bear towel, the way his dad says hello over and over when he wakes up to make him laugh. We are going to the appointments. They're long but not too much to handle, most of the time, and I am listening to a book on tape at night while I pump, to take my mind off the work of it. Jack smiles constantly and hates to fall asleep, especially when he most needs to. Isn't that strange and endearing? His favorite songs are always the ones about you. I love to go on walks by the river with my family, now, up to the bridge where the train roars above us and ducks swim along searching for spring. It is cold some mornings but not too cold and Preston is going to plant seeds soon in raised beds.

I would like to say, *Jesus, thank you*, and *I love you*.

★ ★ ★

Months after Jack was born, months after the surgery, when the drive to Temple was as ordinary as morning coffee, a friend posted the first shudderingly beautiful pictures of her baby after his birth. He was perfect, she said, and he was. All those tiny limbs and wide eyes and the brightness of someone so newly come from God. All the wonder and lightness of his being.

I felt it then, only briefly, a stirring of the old grief. The old grief, that is, of the story that wasn't ours.

How her baby, so bright and fierce and free of tubes, is snuggled up next to her, can go home in his newborn clothes. The old grief that laced in the fabric of our Facebook posts, our introductions of Jack, pleas for help paying his medical bills, petitions for prayers about surgeries, the, as one commenter put it, "embracing of a significant physical disability." The river that runs through our lives is this unusual newness, this life and Jack's wild goodness. Trailing behind it are our unsteady companions, worry and fear, disappointment and confusion, faith that is yielding to the revelation that perhaps God is not understandable, at all.

My grief is a mystery to me, fading and resurfacing as the days slip by. For I do not grieve my son, his disability, the changes of my life. I grieve the narrative where Jesus stops at our house and does a work in me. I grieve the certainty of his arm in my life. I grieve the photos of Jack breastfeeding and going home in newborn clothes and pressing himself into a world all too eager for his brightness, the lightness of his being. This grief is terrible to name, but I name it anyway. What else can I do? I keeled over the other night in front of Jack's crib, both of us crying hard and fast, the slim wooden bars of his crib separating our worlds and our sorrows. Were we crying for the same thing, for a comfort that hadn't been found? Were we both crying out of a longing for sleep, for eyelids that closed and opened onto an easier world? How can I be comfort for Jack when I can find no comfort? How can I give him sleep and an easier world when mine has been lost?

Yet I do. How can this be?

Chapter 11

GOING HOME

I became an apologist for Christianity at fifteen. There weren't many Christians at my small high
school, and so I made it my mission early on to sit in the
thick armchairs at the Starbucks near campus with people
and bridge the gap. I wanted to prove that Christianity
was true—I don't know if it was about them, or about
me. I don't know if I worried much about whether my
friends met Jesus—I was the girl of tenets, logic, of God
distant and omnipotent, of Nicene Creed and the long
history of believers. I thought in arguments and proofs,
not boats on the water in the middle of the night. I
thought in logic, but not in story.

Once when I was in one of these conversations, a
woman who had been eavesdropping on our conversation

came over to me. She leaned in, her voice hushing like wind after a rainstorm. "Here," she said, handing me a Bible. "You're doing a really good job." I thanked her, confused. It didn't occur to me that I had been arguing for God without the Bible, even as I held the book in my hands, turned it over, opened it to the familiar red-letter sections. It didn't occur to me that I hadn't once asked anyone to read the Bible with me, that in my all-consuming love of proving a point I had forgotten that I believed in things that the heart knows often long before the mind. The truth steals up alongside us and taps us on the shoulder, and there I was forcing it into headlong battle.

This is how I moved through my life in the years before Jackson, though I'm sure threads of it were already coming undone before that positive pregnancy test. I moved through the world longing for certainty, lingering in hallways waiting to walk into my next class, my next job, my next friendship. I sought Catholicism for its towering duomos and dogmas; I sought Eastern Orthodoxy for its age and the incense that left holiness residue on your skin; I went back to being Anglican because I was surest of it, surest of God in it. Before Jackson, I went on long runs through the trails behind Gordon College praying, praying, praying for wisdom and guidance and gift and grace, praying for other people in that easy way where I told God I trusted him with whatever was and must be, whatever he was doing, the *He* capitalized in my prayers to show I knew whom to reverence.

And then there was a phone call, nowhere to walk in my building not to be overheard, no way to cry on the phone to the nurse practitioner I didn't even like that much, who'd only heard our baby's heartbeat twice, who didn't know what we'd named him. And in those twenty minutes I wonder if you could have heard it, the slamming of the door as each certainty got up and left me behind. I wonder if you could have heard the fact that I didn't capitalize anything when I prayed to God to tell me that this wasn't real, that he hadn't allowed this to happen to my baby.

While we were back in Boston, a friend from those high school days asked what I was learning, with everything that was happening around me and to me. "About the goodness and love of Jesus," I said. She nodded slowly, her fingers moving up and down, swirling the condensation on her cup. I stammered and lost my train of thought, so new to saying Jesus's name out loud in that Starbucks when it wasn't under the safe cover of a mentoring meeting or a study group for the history of American Christianity. My friend didn't say much, and we eventually changed the subject. I could hear the echoes of my high school self reprimanding me for not offering her all the shiny new arguments I'd learned in graduate school: fine-tuning, free will defense, principle of sufficient reason, first cause and how prior probabilities shift and evolve as we gather evidence. I could feel the woman pressing the Bible into my hands. I wondered if I would ever do a good job again, telling people about Christianity, when those doctrines and towering cathedrals and the holy smell of incense had left me waiting for an explanation I already knew I wouldn't accept, even if I received it.

For those days of ultrasounds, of news and more news, of high-risk pregnancy and eager fetal movement, they wrenched from my hands the proofs of God. It should have been easy to give him up altogether. It should have been easy to release Christianity, the church, the banners and flags of the long line of believers. And yet I still spoke of Jesus in that Starbucks, and I speak his name still, calling out for him, and believing that the Name should still be capitalized.

Living in the NICU, and in the new world that surrounds it, I was hammered thin until I couldn't find it, that core self of iron and certainty and righteousness. I couldn't find that young, eager believer, the unopened Bible in her hands ready to prove that *it simply couldn't be the case that Buddhism and Christianity are compatible.* I couldn't find the argument. When I look at my son, all

I find is his smile running through my life like so much silver fishing wire, thin and terribly strong. When I look for the argument, I see only two cardinals at my window squabbling, a song that will delight Jack when he wakes up from a nap to hear it. When I look for proof, for the reasons, there is nothing to speak back: no objections, no arguments, no neat lines of print marching down the page. The truth walks alongside us through dark hallways labeled "ATU" and "Genetics." The truth walks into operating rooms where a surgeon cuts and lifts skin so tender it tears and rebuilds with every new skill, sitting up or rolling over or crawling. The truth walks, and keeps walking, down the unlit streets of the future where the arguments can't follow. And week by week, ultrasound by ultrasound, I walked after him, and the arguments scattered in his wake.

★ ★ ★

"But you don't understand—I read the directions twice and I washed them on cold and put them on tumble dry low and they SHRANK anyway! I am going to be a terrible mother."

"Stellar logic, Hil." My husband sat on our bed, surrounded still by the brown moving boxes, staring in disbelief and a bit of amusement as I sobbed while laying five Gerber onesies labeled "0–3 months" lovingly across the newly set up Pack 'n Play in our room. Embarrassed that I was thirty-six weeks pregnant and bawling over baby clothes, I got angry.

"You don't get it. I am going to be a terrible mother! How did I already shrink these clothes? How did I not anticipate that they would run small because I just looked on a blog and they said never ever put baby onesies in the dryer because they shrink. I am so stupid! And why did I never do research about what kind of sheets you are supposed to put in a baby crib?!"

It was just one month before my son was supposed to be born, and I held up the little pale blue and green and brown shirt, a friendly lion and mouse print running over it. I rattled it through the air. This, this was the conclusive proof: The test of motherhood—the prewashed onesie— was now so small I could fit it over my hand.

Preston, unfazed, told me to get a grip and drink some water. I huffed into the nursery and shut the door, but of course the door didn't shut all the way, so it sprang back open, which only made me angrier. I sat down on the air mattress that was left over from my friend Lisa's weekend visit and prepared to have myself a good pity party.

As I sat down, the mattress, which was losing air slowly since we had left it up for days, bent under me just enough that a box of bright yellow, red, and green plastic toys fell on top of me. I lay back. A teetering pile of baby towels fell onto my head. The stack of cards that were neatly organized for optimal thank-you note writing slipped off the edge and I heard the whoosh of them going across the smooth wood floor to the other side of the room. No one warned me that I would become a beached whale at the end of pregnancy, and getting out of bed, off the couch, or even out of a vaguely reclining position in a chair would require me to roll onto my side, my feet dangling off the edge, and roll off the surface into a standing position. Thus I was lying, helpless to even do this rolling maneuver, quite literally buried in piles of wipes, teethers, diapers, cloth diapers (because I had thought I wanted to do that, before the night nurse, before everything changed), stuffed animals, and so many children's books it would take the length of a desk and two bookcases to store them all. Jack elbowed me in the ribs.

I started to laugh. I had shrunk all Jack's Gerber onesies and my life was already over in terms of motherhood, and now that I had lain down, the air mattress wouldn't let me get up. I laughed and laughed.

Why am I writing this story? Why is this moment something I remember, over and above all the others? I think about Sarah laughing, first in disbelief and then in joy. Maybe there was disbelief at the end, and joy at the beginning, hidden underneath the others. I think about how Jesus must have made his disciples laugh, how that was a ministry of his too. What do we think he was doing when the little children ran up into his lap? What do we think he meant when he told us not to worry, told us about lilies of the field and birds of the air? I think Jesus gave us laughter. I think Jesus laughed with those children clambering up and getting dirt on his robe and probably in his hair. I think Jesus laughed and scooped those children up and hugged them until they could not ever doubt again that they were each his complete favorite creation, each a singular pearl of great value.

I need it to be written down: There were moments like this, as Jack's arrival came closer and closer to us, when I laughed as I had never laughed before. There were these moments when I was not far from what other people experience in becoming a parent, but I was in their midst, in the depths and pits and wonders with them. There are at least enough other mothers who have accidentally shrunk Gerber onesies in an attempt to be "on top" of prewashing the baby's clothes that there were four separate blog threads discussing how terrible the Gerber sizes were and how much these moms wished they would size bigger. And that August afternoon I was among them, my belly hiding the same complete favorite creation of God, myself, even, a favorite creation too.

Again, the kingdom of heaven is like a merchant in search of fine pearls; on finding one pearl of great value, he went and sold all that he had and bought it. Or what woman, having ten silver coins, if she loses one of them, does not light a lamp, sweep the house, and search carefully until she finds it? When she has found it, she calls together her friends and neighbors, saying, "Rejoice with me, for I have found the coin that I had lost." Just so, I tell you, there is joy in the presence of the angels of God over one sinner who repents.

I still cry to think of it: We are, each of us, the one sinner, the one coin, the pearl of great price. Each of us, the source of unthinkable joy in heaven. Each of us, the treasure God gives everything to redeem.

★ ★ ★

"Do you believe I can still hear God?" I asked Preston on a drive from Temple, the long back roads, through Moody and Woodway, along farm-to-market roads or highways with long strings of numbers. I fiddled with my hands, snapping a hair elastic against my wrist. Preston didn't hesitate. "Yes." I felt the lump in my throat rise up, to fight my words, what I wanted to say and dreaded saying. I changed the subject, drew us back into the past, to the summer before Jack. "I thought I had heard God so clearly. I thought I heard God say he would heal Jack. That he already had."

You know this about me by now: I didn't really believe in miracles anymore. I didn't believe in the healings, the stories, the I-went-to-Mozambique-and-saw-it-with-my-own-eyes. I was too lazy to believe in an alternative explanation and too busy to stop and think about why someone would make up a story like that, but the work of belief I left for others to do. I have lived my life in pursuit of God, so I have said. But there are dimensions I haven't touched, places I haven't put my hands.

In college I had what I thought I understood to be a spiritual awakening. I would creep into the dark chapel auditorium on Sunday nights for the candlelit acoustic worship service—Catacombs, it was called—and I would lift my hands like the others around me. I would close my eyes and lift up my hands and wave them through the air, distracted by how thick the air could feel, how the chapel was especially warm on winter nights. I would close my eyes and hum along since I didn't know the words. This girl fed on the hymns of old, this girl who now calls up six verses of "The King of Love My Shepherd Is." I thought this is what it meant to have a heart after God.

In those days I hungered after many wrong loves, filled my belly with good grades and kisses on the edge of campus three weeks before graduation with a boy who probably couldn't say why he was willing to risk being caught kissing me. In those days I thought I understood that my heart was one hungry for love, for God, and I sometimes thought love and God might be the same thing, that when I felt loved, and beautiful, and real, there God was. When I felt lonely and unseen, there God was not.

These were the dimensions I walked along, all the way up until those positive pink lines, all the way up past them, all the way up to the diagnosis. Why seek God outside where you've found him? Why risk upsetting the spiritual awakening you're so sure you've begun? Why attempt to believe bigger things, when the risk is so much greater than the reward?

"Do you believe I can still hear God?"

Because I don't, I want to scream, because I dreamt night after night of a boy who had two eyes being presented to me by Jesus. Because I said out loud, "If these dreams aren't from you, stop them. Can't you at least stop them?" I don't believe my heart knows the taste of God, because what I ate all those weeks seems like it came to nothing. Because I prayed night after night and Jesus seemed to say that he had already healed Jack. I held my breath in church to keep from crying and I sang the praise songs from college. I closed my eyes and felt the air thick through my fingers again. I walked the dimension of stories where the last line was "And God did the impossible for my daughter, for my son," and I wrote that into my heart for Jack and for myself.

It's so much easier to think that I was wrong to try believing in miracles. If I do that, I don't have to forgive God for withholding the miracle from me.

I meant to say *from Jack*, but I keep failing to write it that way. It says something, doesn't it? I accuse God of withholding the miracle from me, for not rewarding me for the risk of believing. I hide behind Jack in the throne room, hold him out before God as the justification for my disappointment. Jack, whose miracle it should have been. Jack, who's already had miracle sewn into his skin, hour after hour under bright lights and anesthesia. Jack, who has been a miracle all along.

"Do you believe I can still hear God?" I asked again, and again Preston said, "Yes."

"Do you want to hear what I think God just said to me?" I whispered, the lump in my throat giving way. Preston nodded. "God said, 'Hilary, you've been so concerned that Jack will share in suffering and that you can't keep him from his share of suffering. But don't you dare keep him from sharing in my victory.'"

We didn't speak again for a long while. We clenched our knuckles white against the hot black cloth of the passenger seat and wept.

★ ★ ★

Before Jackson was born, we filled the car with praise music. Preston introduced me to the Bruce Springsteen version of "This Little Light of Mine" and I would sing it, my left hand snapping to the beat. We listened to contemporary music. We listened to the black gospel choirs and the crooning Christian guys. These were stored up like promises, chips to cash in later with Jesus. I tallied up my praises because, as Preston would remind me, they go up like incense, a fragrant offering that's pleasing to God. I mostly prayed that these songs would be praises enough to merit the healing.

We spent the first forty-three nights of our son's life sleeping in a different building. We spent the first forty-three days of our son's life beginning and ending our days in the car. We played songs from musicals like *Hamilton*, and we played Taylor Swift. I was so angry with God for changing the world, for leading me out into waters of believing only to change what I was being asked to believe.

I remember wondering if I would ever feel like Jack's mother. Before his tracheostomy surgery, the residents came by with consent forms for anesthesia, for surgery, for a blood transfusion in case he needed one. They told me the risks and I had to swallow hard, signing away all the control I'd managed to gather in the few weeks of living in that uncomfortable chair, living by the breast pump, the granola bars, the large cup of water I never finished. I signed the papers and held Jack. I thought about how the only thing that made me feel like his mother in this building was the fact that they came to me with the papers, that it was me they needed to sign him away. The only thing that made me feel like his mother was writing the word itself on the paper—*mother*—not the weight of him against my chest. He felt like a stranger I was desperately in love with, who might never know my name, my smell, who couldn't taste me or understand me, who woke up in the night to strangers and nurses who changed every twelve hours. But the nurses couldn't sign their names to his consent forms. So I must be his mother.

I was angry at God for changing me too. If you've walked hospital hallways, you know that your self leaches out of you and into the chasms of clockless rooms, that when you go home you're not sure what is left for you, let alone someone you love. I remember this vividly, falling into the white sheets and thin blankets of our hotel. I was not enough for my husband. I had nothing left to give him, and he would still wake up in the middle of the night sometimes to sit with me while I pumped; he would sit at the desk with the tiny hotel lamp and pour the milk into 60 mL containers and stick labels on them and put them in the fridge, and in the freezer when the fridge overflowed. He even convinced the lactation department at the hospital to extend my rental of the hospital pump when we realized the pump my insurance had provided wouldn't handle my oversupply enough to keep mastitis at bay.

All this anger at God brought a long silence, a death and resurrection of belief. All this change brought me to my knees without anything to say. For nine months of pregnancy it felt as though every breath was prayer, or begging. And then for forty-three days and then for more days and weeks and months the words faded to nothing, to echoes of things I had once believed but now could not be sure of.

★ ★ ★

I wrote a blog post just a few weeks before Jack was born, asking people to get out on the water with me and pray. I asked people to show up, boats left far behind, and see Jesus so near us we could touch him, the Jesus who walks on water, the Jesus who heals. I asked these anonymous readers to leave the reasonable behind and pray for the miraculous physical healing in my son, the miraculous in their own lives. This was my confession. I finally believed that Jesus could be that close, that physical, that near. He could do immediately what nature normally does. He could grow an eye or ear; he could close a cleft; he could bring Jackson into the world without needing any help. I believed so hard I crushed the belief in my fingers, my grip so tight. I would not let go of the hope. "The hem of his robe is wide, Hilary, and we are clinging to it. Many, many, many are clinging to it with us." My mother told me this almost every time we talked that summer.

Seven months later, I sat in the dining room, listening to Jack cough in his nursery as he fought with himself to sleep. I held out my hands to Preston. "I just need Jesus to show up for me, no miracles in his hands, no healing." When did I lose my grip on the hem of that robe? When did I let go of that belief about *immediately*? Was it the nights without a nurse, walking back and forth along the creaking floorboards at 4:00 a.m. to see if he was still breathing? Was it the third trip to Temple in a week, to check the G-button, to check granulation tissue? Was it the realization that Jack hadn't gone outside more than a handful of times because the flu can travel up to nine feet and the PICU is not a place to raise a baby? Was it all of it, and none of it?

I held out my hands and twisted them into my lap, falling silent too quickly. Preston had to teach his class on the spiritual disciplines. It was the week of the examen, the prayer of self-examination at the end of the day, the prayer that distinguishes our mistakes from our sins, the prayer that asks, "Where did you feel close to Jesus to-day?" I lingered in the living room, listening as Preston led his group through the prayer. Where have I felt close to Jesus?

★ ★ ★

I sing Jack hymns to help him fall asleep. I sing him down to the river to pray; I sing in the sweet by and by; I sing abide with me.

There is the robe, the song, "In life, in death, abide with me." Where am I close to Jesus? Walking those floorboards singing Jack to sleep, my hand on his chest to feel him breathe. In the car every time we drive home from Temple, from every routine appointment we never asked to have, passing the exits where we prayed, where we imagined, where we believed. In the realization that Jack and I sat on the porch the other day, the sun and leaves gentle and kind and green to us, the air sweet, and Jack fell asleep drooling onto my chest the way I begged God once that he would, that bit of normal, that bit of grace.

★ ★ ★

When I talk to Jesus now, I tell him about the woman suffering from hemorrhages. I tell him about her prayer, her work of belief; it was reaching out just for the hem of his robe. I tell him about how so much of me gave up even waiting to see if he would walk by. I ask him where he was, all those days and nights whose hours I cannot number.

Jesus reminds me that the woman reached out for his robe. She reached and in reaching she linked herself to Jesus, even as he was walking somewhere else. I just need Jesus to show up. And there is his robe around the corner, down the hallways, and now if I close my eyes, I can almost feel the cloth in my hands. Jesus holds out the wide hem of his robe and gives me the way to reach back.

Epilogue

OUT IN THE JORDAN

Sometime before his first birthday, in the height of the Texas summer, I forgot to sing Jack to sleep. He wanted to stay up and play, or he wanted silence, his head resting heavy on a shoulder. He tended to prefer his dad's, so I was often ushered out of the room and told to take a break. I cleaned the kitchen relentlessly, thrusting clean mugs and glasses into their respective places, sweeping rooms that needed no sweeping. What was I looking for? How did such restlessness linger, while my son raced ahead, his eyes fixed on the fullness of his ever-expanding world?

Jack got tracheitis, a specific bacteria building up on his trach when it would in other bodies be contained in the ebb and flow of the symbiotic bacteria in the lungs.

He never seemed sick, but he fussed at nap time, reluctant to sleep away from us, and as hungry as I was for every minute of his skin on mine, I relented, day after day, curling up on the couch or in the chair that I always imagined belonged to the nurses, not the mother. He wanted me to sing again. I tried hymn after hymn, but the only one that worked, the one that kept us and keeps us still, was "Poor Wayfaring Stranger."

My son must know, in the words of St. Augustine, that we are restless until we rest in Jesus. My son must know that life is a rising up, a complaint and an exhortation and a song sent before the throne of God. My son must know that throne is reached through the Jordan River. And so when I sing, he settles in. When I sing, I settle in too.

All rivers run to a sea somewhere. All rivers move to something bigger and wilder. The Jordan is no different, the waters no less cold or fierce or frightening. But when we wade in, so far that our feet can't touch the bottom, there we find Jesus. There we find voices to speak the unimaginable. There we find a great wave of forgiveness pushing us out and up. There I found my son's head resting heavy on my shoulder as I carried us slowly into the arms of Jesus. And there, at the beginning of a life I had never imagined, in the depths of a river I prayed to cross over unchanged, I found our God.

Acknowledgments

A special thank-you to my husband, who pushed me to write this book and believed in it long before I did, and to Jack and June, the mischievous, daring, curious, creative, wildly joyful children that you are—for teaching me how to be a mom. A tremendous thank-you to my family—Mom, Dad, Roger, Pauline, Abby, Sam, Joe, Joel, Mariah, and my wonderful nieces and nephews—for the grace, peace, and joy you carry alongside us as we walk this road together.

Thank you, Lisa, for listening to me pace the NICU floors for hours on the phone, flying to see us even for two-day visits, and holding every one of my questions up to the light with me.

Thank you, Lily, Abigail, Charity, and Cherie, for your front porches, afternoon coffees, spontaneous playdates, and ceaseless encouragement, for how you show love and care to me in a thousand small ways. Thank you, Caroline and Heidi, for making the space for me to learn who

I most wanted to be, and Sharon, Elaine, and Agnes, for abiding in the mystery of God with me.

Thank you to my wonderful agent, Angela, and my editor, Virginia, for keeping me truthful and brave, and for making this story so much richer in its telling, and to the folks at Hachette and FaithWords, for diving in with me and believing in this book. My thanks for the many, many people who made this book possible—my thankfulness far outstrips the space I have here.

About the Author

HILARY YANCEY loves good words, good questions, and sunny afternoons sitting on her front porch with a strong cup of tea. She and her husband, Preston, and their two children, Jack and Junia, live in Waco, Texas, where Hilary is completing her PhD in philosophy at Baylor University.